The Cabinet of Traces

3

Introduction 7–9

The Cabinet of Traces
Alan Quireyns 11–15

Personal Details
Koen Sels 17–32

Traces 33–179

Pedigrees of Objects
Interview with
Clémentine Deliss
181 – 192

Index of Artists
2013 – 2018
193 – 201

Index of Activities
2013 – 2018
203 – 221

INTRODUCTION

The Cabinet of Traces is an initiative by AIR Antwerpen vzw. Artists in Residence Antwerp organizes living - and working periods for visual artists from and in Antwerp, Belgium, Europe and the rest of the world. These artists are invited for residency periods between three and six months, where flexibility and independency are the guiding principles. The artists chose themselves how they want to fill in the residency and the team of AIR Antwerpen supports them in all possible ways.

The Cabinet of Traces is part of the perennial archival project *AIR Traces.* In 2012 AIR Antwerpen published under the same title a publication with an overview of its residents and activities between 2005 and 2012. Then The Cabinet of Traces also originated, existing out of traces consciously left behind. In 2014 AIR Antwerpen organized the group exhibition *AIR Traces: Austruweel* in and around the old lockkeeper's house in the harbor of Antwerp. Fourteen visual artists presented on seven different locations existing and new works, departing from the traces they found in this unique environment.

The goal of *AIR Traces* is to visualize the activities during the residency. Most of these activities are part of the inspiration - and thinking process of the artist and ephemeral in character. The result of a residency is often only seen after the residency period has ended. The Cabinet of Traces thus asks the question what remains in the studio when the artist has left. The studio considered as the place where the artist works and lives, exceeding the borders of the room, extending into the city and the socio-cultural context. The traces in this book represent the interaction between living and working that is the essence of a residency.

The Cabinet of Traces includes traces from 2013 to 2018. Until 2016 AIR Antwerpen was located in the old lockkeeper's house and moved its premises to the former officers houses at the Kielsevest in the south of Antwerp. By the end of 2018 AIR Antwerpen moves to its final destination: the abbot's house in the old Dominican monastery at the Ploegstraat, behind the zoo of Antwerp in the area of the central station. There *AIR Traces* will start a new chapter. From then onwards every artist in residence will create an intervention with a copy of this publication, so the Cabinet of Traces continues to grow.

The Cabinet of Traces exists out of three parts. The first part includes the introduction and texts by Alan Quireyns and Koen Sels. *The Cabinet of Traces* gives an insight into the original thoughts that formed this publication and is written by artistic director Alan Quireyns. It shares thoughts about the residency format and the relationships between humans and objects, memory, the process of photography and the archive. The text *Personal Details* by novelist Koen Sels is inspired on some of the objects in the collection and the uniqueness of the artist in residence at large. The second part of the publication exists out of the collection of 73 traces, collected between 2012 and 2018, including technical details, the name of the artist, and a title. The third part is a chapter with source material. It includes an interview with freelance curator and former director of the Weltkulturenmuseum

Frankfurt Clémentine Deliss. The interview delves into the relationship between ethnographic collections and contemporary art, the use of residencies in this context and how a possible future growth of anthropologic collections could look like. This interview was a big inspiration for the production of The Cabinet of Traces. The source chapter also includes an index of all artists in residence between 2013 and 2018 and a list of activities in the same period. This material allows to have an overview of how the residency functions, which artists were involved and how the traces relate to them.

THE CABINET OF TRACES

A hallway. A door. A man with his eye to the spyhole, head tilted, hands cupped on either side, peering through. Silently, holding his breath, looking into a room. What he sees looks further away than it really is.

He sees a table, and stooping over it a human shape. He reads its attitude, its expression, its activity. He sees a physical presence, nothing more. A shuffling male figure: he knows neither the language the man speaks nor his origin. On the table: strips of wood, bits of string, paper, glue. Here and there, a carelessly hung drawing. An unmade bed, a half-open cupboard.

Now the shape straightens up and walks towards the lens. The watcher freezes; his cheeks burn. For a heartbeat he thinks the door's going to open and he'll be caught standing there with his hands still in the air. But no—next to the door there's another cupboard, from which the man fetches a ruler. Silently our observer turns his head and disappears towards the stairs.

The spyhole was the doing of visual artist Nicholas Hoffman, who purposely fitted it back to front in the door of studio no. 3 on the second floor of the lock-keeper's house. The spyhole installation was originally part of an Open Studios event for which Hoffman was unavoidably absent. On the outside of the door he hung a photocopied image of a collection of plastic coffee cups, seen from above. In the centre of the image one cup stood upright; in the middle of that cup was the spyhole. Presented like this the hole exerted a phenomenal power of attraction, sucking you in much as the rabbit hole swallowed up Alice. When I looked through it I saw a miniature version of Hoffman's studio, which he'd built on the other side. It had a feel of an animated movie—any second you expected its bustling little resident to appear. During the Open Studios all I saw was the scale model, not the real studio. A double reversal, as it were. I expected to see authenticity, the artist behind the artwork, and got a facsimile instead. With this little intervention Nicolas Hoffmann transformed the private space into an artificial public space.

Hoffman's spyhole lived on. When the question came to leave something deliberately behind in the residency, he named it *Before Breakfast* and the intervention became part of The Cabinet of Traces as catalogue no. 25. The Cabinet of Traces is a collection of seventy-three traces that were left by the artists who stayed in the residence between 2013 and 2018. At the start of their stay I asked them to leave something consciously behind when their time here came to an end. There were several things that prompted me to do this, among them Orhan Pamuk's writing, more particularly his *Museum of Innocence.* The book tells the story of a man who becomes a compulsive collector of objects related to his dead beloved. He wallows in these things, living among them, trying thus —though in vain—to regain his lost love. The consolation the objects offer can only ever be superficial, but even though they sit immobile in their places they evoke memories through which the couple's story and the beloved's sad death can be reconstructed. Pamuk himself was unable to resist the lure of those objects, which he collected in reality, acquiring them from junk shops and antique dealers in Beyoğlu, Istanbul. Orhan Pamuk could not resist to imitate reality even further and installed an actual Museum of Innoncence, where the objects on display are arranged according to the chapters of the book.

As humans we can't help but give objects added meaning. In reality they're inanimate and void, but via our own agency we connect them with particular people and their habits. We read them like a user's guide in order to get to know someone. We cherish them for the sake of the memories that adhere to them. We try to say something with the objects we give each other or display in our living rooms. Surrounding ourselves with particular objects enables us quickly to adapt, to move from one situation to another. They pacify us, remind us who we are. They calm us down.

Children are experts in acknowledging the importance of objects. Appropriation even precedes talking as they seize on certain objects like a cuddly toy or a blanket. It enables them to exercise a particle of control in a world that is completely filled by the things of others. What they do with these objects is largely decided by themselves. They enable them to keep a check on their fear of the outside world and so to move from a familiar context into the great unknown.

The traces presented in this book form a strange collection of objects, drawings, small works of art, letters and items of clothing. Often, residents opted for an item derived from something that took place in the residence, a souvenir. Some chose to make something new, specifically for this collection. And others presented a personal item, something they'd worn next to their skin. Every object tells a tale, some more exciting than others, some sadder, some funnier. These anecdotes are not related here per se, but you can hear their whispers. Some are true, some hearsay, some an amalgam of rumour and legend. The stories that orbit around these traces lead a life of their own. To write them down is to imprison them.

The art of storytelling originated with the traveller. A residency, in which a resident artist is per se a traveller, is a place of stories par excellence. The Cabinet of Traces recalls those tales but is also the seedbed for new ones. Hopefully it'll cause some good-natured bickering about what actually happened, what this or that object was used for, how it was made, and who it belonged to. Memories are constructions and the traces in this book are the building blocks, wheels, joints and connecting rods with which those memories can be created. The Cabinet of Traces is a construction kit that frees the imagination. It's a tool that fuels the mind's invention. The book will be passed on to future artists in residence, who'll react to it in their turn. They'll expand the collection. They'll add something to it, criticize it, destroy it or decorate it.

The Cabinet of Traces exists only in the shape of photographic reproduction. Photos uproot. They're a form of transport and an expression of absence. They separate the objects from the context in which they originated. Like the catalogue of an ethnographic collection, standard information accompanies each trace: the material used, the size, a title (in some cases), and the name of the artist. The objects were photographed against a plain white background in a photographic studio. The background neutralizes, it eliminates the original context. Though there are a few cases this wasn't possible. The traces left on the residency building itself, or somewhere in the city, could not be neutralized so easily. Hence the recognizable bits of the city, of a building, a door, a staircase, a window, an attic.

In The Cabinet of Traces there's no mention of where someone comes from. There's no reference to the journeys the objects undertook to become part of the collection. The reader can fill that in for himself. What remains is the artist and the artistic act that is linked to the leaving of a conscious trace. Thus The Cabinet of Traces gives everyone the same starting point, whether they come from Frankfurt or Tijuana, Liège or Tehran. Maybe if you approach the objects as a person you'll be able to coax the stories from them. Then they detach themselves from their thing-ness.

Just like the imagination of the silent visitor breathlessly peering into the room, the meaning of this collection is created by what you don't see. In the objects' simplicity vast universes are latent. They triumph over time and the uncertain whims of their owners. Collecting is motivated by the need to combat the fragmentation of the world, its distention in time and space. Objects mark moments. They derive their status from their relationship with a particular moment in life, an event. They form a memory, a remedy against dispersal.

Alan Quireyns

PERSONAL DETAILS

Far from Vilnius, Bucharest or Sidney, in a bend of the Scheldt river, which was, in a way, close to itself, I mean was self-evident, gathered under the auspices of the liberal arts, with cups of wine, we talked in 2016 about the transience of things and the changing artistic landscape, about the Internet and food. There were so many ugly things, was one of the opinions a person inevitably expressed in that context, but ugliness simply had no critical function anymore in the post-internet age. And anyone in the group who happened to have the same opinion, felt they were becoming old, passé and whiny, accused himself even before being accused by another person, which always happened, and then you could no longer cover yourself with your self-awareness and perspective, then there you were, assuming a position. The country of Belgium was so strange, another person said, a psychotic and yet warm confusion, an identity crisis in the form of a country, we all thought the inhabitants were so difficult to read, so neurotic. There was consensus, even the Belgians themselves agreed, as endlessly fascinated as they were by the mirror that only foreigners could hold up to them. We had only been here months or even weeks. The experience of working days was necessarily vague. There was no conversational form, for ideas that arose during the shower or at breakfast or the afternoon nap, so we sometimes felt unmentionably lonely. Until, working on something alone or jointly on a text or work or something, or an idea or an evening, we felt connected again, not just subjective and sick and incomprehensibly alone. Every discourse was recognised by all of us in advance, that was how we had been brought up, we were always separate from everything, separate from what was direct, unmediated and clear, separate from ourselves. The sun never disappeared, it was only blocked or hidden by fog or clouds. The weather forecast was constantly updated. The noises of trucks expressed our life the best, another side of the artist's existence. A person tried to include that current, the work produced from it was boring, but that was allowed.

At an opening, A. very purposefully drank away the party of the day before and the nerves of that afternoon. It made his experience of the world, his physical condition and his private thoughts flow into each other. That was allowed without shame, there was and never had been a world possible that remained impersonal and objective, this was the world, subjective and instantaneous, as artists they were always in it, touched everything with their desires and thoughts and that was good, A. himself was only a medium for the world, an input and output with organs. Was this withdrawal, these nerves? He had not done anything concrete as a resident, but that was fine, who said he should already produce at what moment, which mechanism his voice belonged to? Hundreds of photographs and notes, still in folders, they would only be edited into an anti-film when he got home again. You could not pronounce that work without another's voice, the open fire of the historic avant-garde. Or was it a photo-essay, they were names like others, he saw himself as a joke, thought it pleasant. To liberate his ideas, he had written a random system on the wall.

Five counts to decide what could and could not: *good good good bad bad.* Below it a photocopy of pipes, with petroleum or natural gas, he was too lazy or maybe just vain enough not to seek it out. Beside it, the Dutch conjugations of to have and to be. He asked B. to pour another one, in a decent continental English, and enjoyed speaking that language fairly well. Then he extended his expressions: 'I forget where I'm from today. It's good though, really nice.'

At the same time, B also poured herself a cup and wasn't sparing with it for once, she thought the evening lay before her today, and she lived up to this gathering of people and it wasn't always like that, sometimes she hated this stuff. She rolled her eyes in a friendly way and drew the attention of A. to his tendency always to talk out of context, which she thought was both strange and likable, she made that clear, but now she wanted to go and stand somewhere else, she said, of course she didn't have to but there were lots of possible conversations today, here, at this point under the gentle summer sun at around six. 'Right.'

C. struggled in that morning, having partied enough and yet not hopelessly drunk, and then to awaken in the very late afternoon, that seems only to be one superficial breath later, to awaken with an unprecedented deep and concrete sense of all-encompassing vagueness, as if it could not even exist in that state and in this place. The sun undoubtedly seems cosmically and inhumanely hard in her eyes while the route home, kilometres along the quays, played again in her head. Not that she thought of it, not intentionally, I mean; it just developed, as if something inside her was thinking. She called a friend and said: 'I don't know, it's like… I don't know, physical.' There was talking outside, it was hypnotic, their voices disengaged from what they said. She deliberately listened to it.

Love was difficult, there was no language for it, D. stuttered, at least not for those who felt the language of love was broken. But love existed, that thought was a kind of base, below which he could fall. He loved camomile tea that someone brought him when he was told that his prints would not be ready. Camomile tea doesn't work, he said, it is soft, but you're also sweet. On Thursday morning, he left off emailing for what it was because an unspecified conversation with Y. was so obvious that he believed that nothing could be more important than continuing it. Half a day of bullshitting, he was up and tense afterwards but it continued to work for a long time and became a memory. Several Antwerp residents walked a little way with him because he had asked the way. They seemed to find nothing more fun than helping tourists.

E. ate a date and put the pit in a jar in which he planted basil seeds that just did not want to germinate. However, when the date subsequently, as a miracle of nature, germinated, that caused a rare, childlike enjoyment. He researched how something grows. A particular focus: for an hour his mind moved as a funnel from that subject to all the other subjects that attracted it, that made his urge to flee disappear or grounded it. It was like drawing but then drawing as he did as a child, separate from everything, before the Internet and the distraction and the undesirable endlessness of everything.

With an almost irritating satisfaction with his thoughts, F. looked at the print his teeth had made on the Snickers Bar he had half-eaten with one bite, because he had already been working hard all day. That brain is thinking in me or something. He smoked a cigarette and drank a coca cola.

We believed that art could, in principle, be anything, we may disagree about the procedures that could give it power as art, but at least we felt connected by tolerance, although we also often fell out, this and that was also said about him or her, primarily to understand who we were ourselves. It rained for weeks and it was the colour of streets made from concrete slabs and the river and air were indistinguishably grey. You couldn't remember the days, not as limited pieces of time. It made us pissed off and bored. Then we fell in a tunnel of identifications and often badmouthed friends and colleagues.

According to G., the Samberstraat is the most normal place. There a girl was talking about the neighbourhood, although the girl didn't know it so well herself. She knew that one was more worth seeing than another. For instance, the Slachthuislaan and the Eilandje were particularly special. G. briefly lost her mental balance walking along the docks. Normality dematerialised, she thought, and then then, goodness what big words, but it was true. Very often she felt that she had to write things down, particularly at random moments, not to forget that life was not a composition of points for attention but rather: road surface, ivy, bread bag, dentist, bus, dog poo, bicycle tyre, chewing gum, rust spot, advertising panel, graffitied dicks. It wasn't unpleasant, that everything was both foreground and background and that the causes and consequences of what she saw only seemed seconds away from being grasped. Everything was a *matter of fact,* a *state of affairs.* And the Eilandje was also quite pretty, there you could see beyond the place before, it was like oxygen.

The materiality of photography was a sinkhole for H.'s thoughts. It was a reality machine, he thought, dilapidated like flying saucers and conspiracies, and just as productive, or otherwise, a counterpart that creates contours. Now he walks in total oblivion as a horizon around the city park and thought about citizenship. In his head it was 1926. He had no idea how and when it became 2016, but something was very different in this age. He was ashamed of the vagueness of his thoughts, of his nostalgia, which was not really thought but was a function of his emotions, ephemeral, passive. It didn't become clearer.

Sadly—I. lost it in the bathroom of his residence in the city where he was born. With a sleepy, unobtrusive, light-hearted, even sweet lucidity, kindled by loud music, he realised his life would be too short to realise his dream of freedom, prosperity and salvation. It was aweful. He felt he had never been allowed to cherish that image for a minute, it was wrong, bad, he should never have wasted time as a Free Artist in the timeless nineties, eighties or seventies, with a cup of beer in his partying hand and euphoria concealed in his heart, dancing for freedom, teenage kicks of a sixteen-year-old, for the pristine possibilities of never sleeping again, of always sleeping. That dream was too old and too stupid for this age. He knew it, he was not stupid, he forgot but then always knew it again. He just never managed to reset himself, he was at stake himself, stood as a society model to social unrest. So what was left to him otherwise, he thought, when he knew it all too well than to defend himself in or from his imagination, which was not an idea but a place, not a solid location but a gentle spatial relationship, a place of noise and body heat in a hammering reality. When drunk he had tried to explain what place it could have been. Then he became one of the many friends at a truly legendary birthday party in 1973 in Café De Tweede Tiet, arguing with a haughty, untouchable laugh with a poet who believed the unremitting labour of the Mind was the most noble, and which he felt were charlatans and a bunch of posers who thought a walk through the park was adequate in the name of contemporary art. A head looking for a punch, another pub-goer said. That kind of thing sharpened his arrogance. His loose face then said ‘beh’, and with a cognac he moved into a higher gear. But he was not sitting in De Tweede Tiet, De Kat or Den Bureau. He had lost his faith in art, could also not drink with the same religious vigour as in the past, could no longer despise life. And yet he still drank, as a renegade, misbegotten nihilist.

J. was able to use a large, industrial hall in the port for a few days. The sun was filtered through hazy windows that formed a narrow strip just under the roof along the entire length of the hall. Coincidentally, the light on that day was following a clear path: changing shapes moved in a semi-circle over the floor, morning and afternoon mirrored each other. There were holes in the roof, it smelled of pigeon droppings. The setting felt intimate, that was the strange thing, it was something to do with being enclosed, the breathing space and the division of the day.

It was hopeless, K. thought, walking along the Kammenstraat. He didn't want to stand out because of his intelligence. Or his complexity. His anger, his humour, his work ethic, his long sentences, his laziness, his tics, his dislike of the babble in doorways or elsewhere, anywhere really, also his simplicity, his difficult mood, his place in the margins, his intuitive sense of what was contemporary and obviously his opposition to it, because it was only a function of who he was, because he was a slave to it. And his silence, his work and his age, and his music, and his tragedy, his excess, his masturbation in the sink, and his awareness of it, his so-called honesty, his tired, beautiful face. Hello squirrel, kid goat, sparrow and miniature horse, he said. And hi asshole with your gossip, come and sit with me, we will sort everything out. And the books he read, the routes he knew passing places he had already been, the texts he wrote for all kinds of publications, the clouds he saw, the mezze he made on New Year's Eve, the fireworks he didn't get because he was 'tired', the drugs he took, the cities he did or didn't like, the enemies he has, the girls he had, the guitars he chose, the people he knew, the photographs from when he was a toddler, the thirteen artists who thought his exhibition was really good, the millions who ignored him, the city where he was born and where the spring always blooms differently than anywhere else, the slightly cooler warmth above the canal in the summer and his impossible sex drive in a past in which he had not yet had sex, with anybody, everybody, it is all the same. His modernity and his idea that he was not of this time. His disappointments and his socialism. The forest edge, börek! His opinions and his facts. His conceptualism and his romanticism. Hi mum, dad. Petrol station, source of oil. His hoarse stuttering and the ease with which he writes. His banality, his depth. His apparently suddenly shrunken penis and his never consummated bisexuality. And authenticity. And freedom. Today, this is all behind him, still just behind him, as the last dull thought of a depression. He didn't even know, that it was already over, now he was always still on the edge of slipping again. There was a bottle of red wine, there were drinkers, K. and L. who were not prone to his torments and cultural pessimism, they were at home with Facebook and Skype, and he was possibly more jealous than angry with them. Nobody forgets more quickly than a person thinking that they have to change now, really change. The Flemish poplars immediately waved that urge away, the wine was still there. His psychology, he thought, was hopeless, but he had some kind of strength in himself.

Going down further and deeper in the siesta, the self-evident and the unbridled slid into each other. They didn't dissolve each other, but wound their nature around and around each other. Thoughts occurred, in a space without centre, without agency. Salvation was the word for the breath-taking drizzle in L.'s head.

Quarter to ten. M. had bought a clock because she couldn't do without one. She had just woken up and looked at it detachedly, didn't read the time and yet it had a narrative function. If she looked back over recent months, she thought in her semi-sleeping state, she had lost all chronology. Everything could have occurred on a well-filled day. She had lost her beacons, and it was as if she could have been many other people, not a painter but a video artist, sculptor, author. The differences were minimal.

N. loved foggy air and the early morning, that was always inhuman and crisp. The fine twilight veil, which is drawn back too slowly and too gradually for human eyes from the country and river, the thick and dark blue, not a tint of cloudy water but an all-encompassing surface, a dark mirror, still now, before the sun did its work with the water. It was already there, just like the moon. It was fully light, but its rays were not yet directly reaching the earth, it was many kilometres further on, but not here, here it barely shone along the crust and back into the cosmos. So the blue sky landed as a fat drop of ink in the hard current, that seemed motionless, not overripe and stagnantly still like objects in the noon light, that was the light of pollution, but glassy, a hardened gelatine of colour resin, iris blue, one of the aggregation conditions of reality, of the perfectly normal day. Demarcations of time slide into each other. Both days and years moved concentrically and invisibly to a central point. The seagulls arrogantly screeching pushed into the living space of the city pigeon, enjoyed their waste and left their droppings. That she was on an edge pleased her, that there would also come a point that day after which nothing was important, caused turmoil. Now the late afternoon was still an eternity away, she was still in the middle of the spring of this completely normal Wednesday and she was surprised to discover this Himalayan pleasure here, in this ugly, oxygen-rich but saturated with fine particles low country without blossoming hills and a real fauna and flora. Together with a fleeting smell of petrol the satanic ideas of industry and activity spread undeniably through the soul of this space, which was not becoming too big, which encompassed the entire world and all its hustle and bustle, and she wanted tea, joined the unspoilt excitement of the early mailers in the kitchen, where another logic applied, where you didn't care about a lack of space and shared bathrooms, because you were an artist and free, of everywhere and nowhere, universally legible and yet mysterious. She took in the morning air and the rest of her joy.

On the night of the nocturnes, O. thought that the mental system that shaped streets, cities, countries and other constellations was more clearly delimited than ever before. Cycling from here to there he located the place of visual arts in the centre of that whole. His mind's eye saw a ritual celebration of repetition and difference, with cables and radar works that connected individuals and groups. He heard scratching and squeaking in uncomfortable silences and discussions, observed an urge to have everything end in a single great party destroying all distances. Through that supercilious role of observer he landed beyond art. He had lost all directness and involvement, not for the first time. Although he already felt connected, through connections and demarcations and presence, he could not be a participant on that day. The miracle of his artistry was also that he was always able to pick up again after those evenings, that he could forget this loss of faith while sleeping. But now he saw nothing other than a machine of opinions and distinctive features, of exhibitions and visitors, of students, former artists and go-getters, from buyers and incidental browsers enjoying the awful free wine. That evening an artist had made an avatar of himself in an awkward computer game without purpose with dancing strippers and harmless monsters, charred sticks were placed on the gallery floor, an abstract expressionist work was exhibited that had been painted in 2014, a press article written about tactile photography as an intimate touch could be read, with a view to the turbulent reality a relevant presentation of a collection and documentary video work could be seen at the museum, the disproportionately intelligent, black-clothed couples untouched by everything and everyone trooped into an art gallery, people could listen to an artist talk with an artist who claimed not to enjoy talking about his work, and there was a chaotic programme in which ad hoc performances and live music got in each other's way so that the energy and good intentions were mainly retained, which was also the organisers' intention. On that kind of event some boys and girls and women and men fell hopelessly in love and O. took that thought into his sleep.

P. put a photocopy of the document from the ethnographic museum on the table, beside the crocodile-shaped ashtray, the stack of romance books, the keys, the framed photograph of his girl-friend and child, the three pens and two pencils, the train ticket, the staff card, and the empty bottle of lemonade and was pleased with the order of things.

Q. slipped although, or just because, she was cycling very carefully through the snow.

And R. laughed and said 'you have to keep cycling, twit' and skidded himself because of it. A joke followed about their Mediterranean background. Through the stupid laughter they deepened their affection for each other. It was a short trip filled with incidents. He wondered whether he would remember it soon or that it would always be there for a lifetime, consciously or subconsciously, like a text that you read a second time years later and that you hadn't remembered at all but of which you perfectly remember the words you read on that page.

S. thought the Belgian was soft and complacent, and then became angry when another person told her that nobody called themselves 'Belgian' here —'Flemish perhaps, but even then.' And it seemed as if nobody ever came into the street in this country, she said in the same conversation, and that there was complete lack of historical awareness. She didn't even mention the word capitalism because what had once been emancipating, was now blinding. She thought. Whether it would lead directly to a dull lethargy, to the greyness of always the same thing again, and she hated the lack of involvement. That evening she fretted over it for a long time. Perhaps her commitment was a narcissistic demarche, could she not see that it was made possible through her privileged position? What if you were a checkout lady, what could you do after working hours? Was she proud and arrogant? Or was her preoccupation with such problems part of the real problem. Shouldn't she think like that? But could you direct thoughts and say: you mustn't think like that? How could one truly be a subject of your thoughts? Cursing the theory, she fell asleep. At 9:00 am she woke up, miraculously more refreshed than ever before. She immediately took up her book and pencil.

T. had already explored the entire area using Google Street View, but as it always turned out, once he was truly there, it only elicited a vague recognition. He was sometimes astounded by it, that the reality was not equally virtual. That was a strange thought, that later proved extremely productive, but at that time hurt a very little bit, that could be forgotten like an image of the clock on your laptop, that said 13:13, doubly unlucky. What does it mean to stay in a place, he wondered in the vaguest of ways, what kind of art is that? Then the thought was buried with other impressions, became a scratch on his day. It was still there, but you consciously had to feel for it to find it.

U. had no interest in contextual art practice, for instance nothing with local histories that were researched for meaningful details, from which a truth spoke that enlightened everything, that came as falling in love, or with cartographies or data or other A4-art, she sometimes used that word, in which patterns waited for the inner eye, for a spectator, she was not like that, she painted, and yet, and yet, when she thought like that, then…

V.'s heart was overflowing. In fact, she had to write a text for a publication, but she was thinking about her new book, always preferred thinking about it than writing, writing was necessary.

Her imagination was warm and liquid: suddenly the text had an attitude, and it remainded her of this: that theme and events were of no importance, as life in itself was of no importance, but that which was told, must be imbued with tone and music. That was no aesthetics, it was a policy of life. She postponed writing, thought about her month old baby, noticed that it was an instrument of her own gaze—she experienced everything double, but this time, the doubling did not hurt. Who cared that it was all fiction, that the child lived on the other side of the words?

It was a reality of stacks, of commas hanging in the air, thought W., but it could have been any other resident who thought this. They are shocking phrases of lived experience, he then said, the intensity, not the accuracy of thoughts, what attached to full consciousness, for instance on a long day when people come together and swarm out in the evenings to the squares and in cafés, and what it leaves behind. We have nothing to prove, we are artists, nobody has to want to be the cleverest or most relevant, we work on experience, beyond good or bad or ugly or beautiful or contemporary and timeless.

And X. agreed and Y. interrupted him, and Z. understood nothing about it, and the differences and origins and sexes and age rearranged themselves and she thought, this constellation in the second decade of the twenty-first century, this art in the spring wind that carries oil and weeds, is a matter of faith, and who knows that faith may already be over, maybe the unstable constellation of practicing the free occupation of artist somewhere as a complete fulfilment of a life without a centre,

perhaps that constellation has already collapsed,
perhaps that history ends here with us in 2016
and she was sad because it might be true.

Koen Sels

TRACES

Fritz Welch
Upside down protest sign (Zabriskie Point)

wall drawing in pencil
420 mm × 297 mm
2011

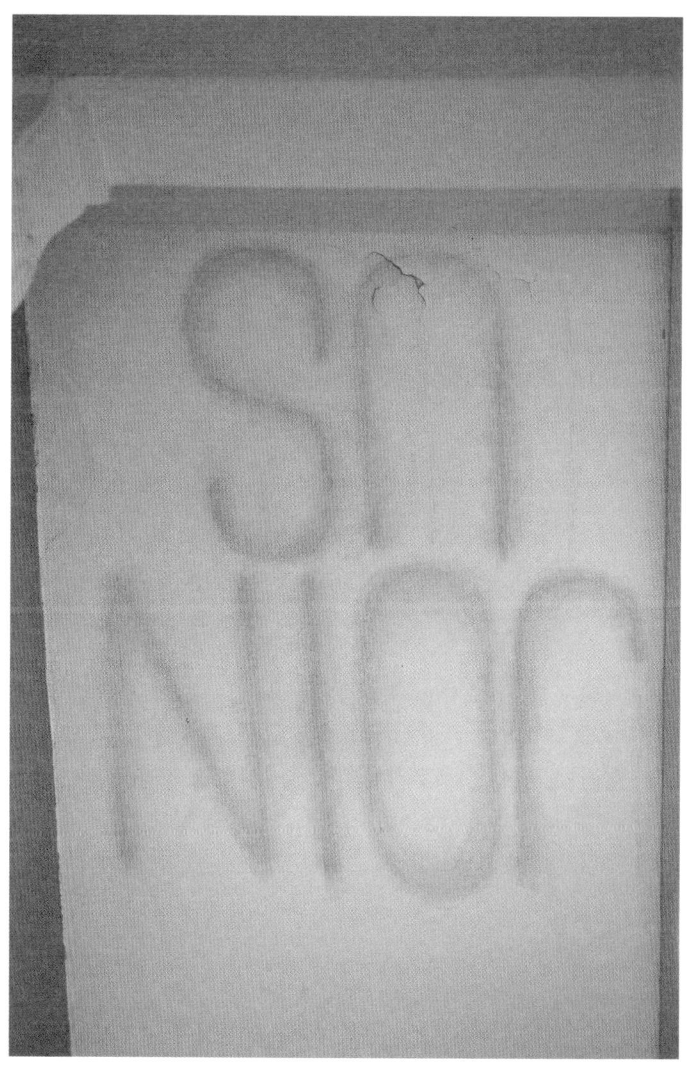

cat. 01

Malthe Stigaard
Thank you note

black ballpoint drawing
297 mm × 210 mm
2012

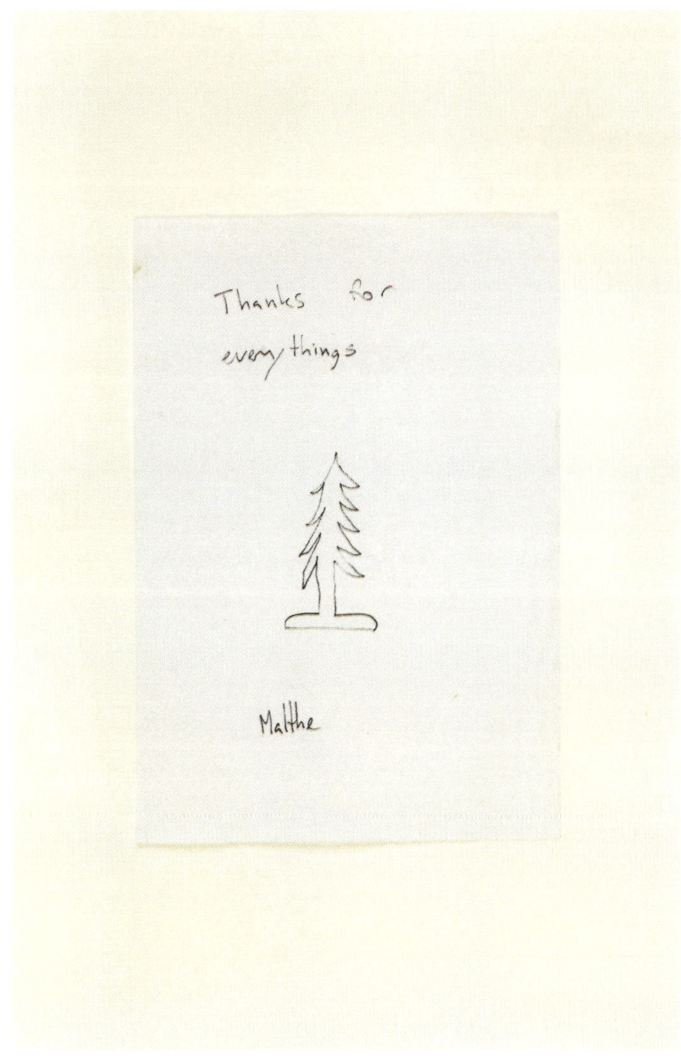

cat. 02

Caner Aslan

reproductions of maps and brochure
367 mm × 288 mm
2012

DE HAVEN VAN ANTWERPEN
NEDERLAND
Het Essentiële
L'Essentiel
The Essential
U Bevindt zich
Hier
ANTWERPEN

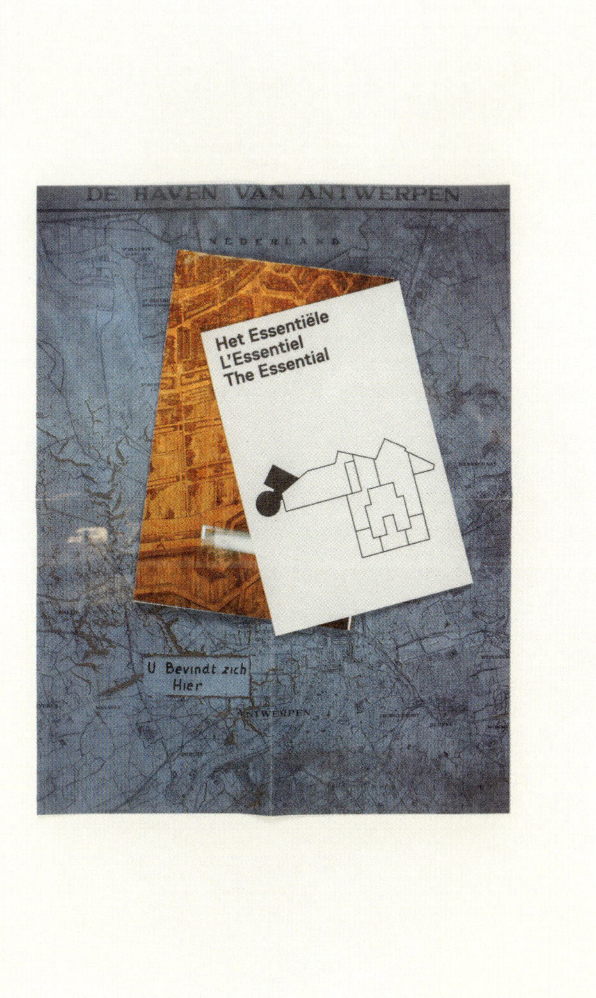

cat. 03

Nina Könnemann
Basketball Towel

terry cloth
180 cm × 100 cm
2009

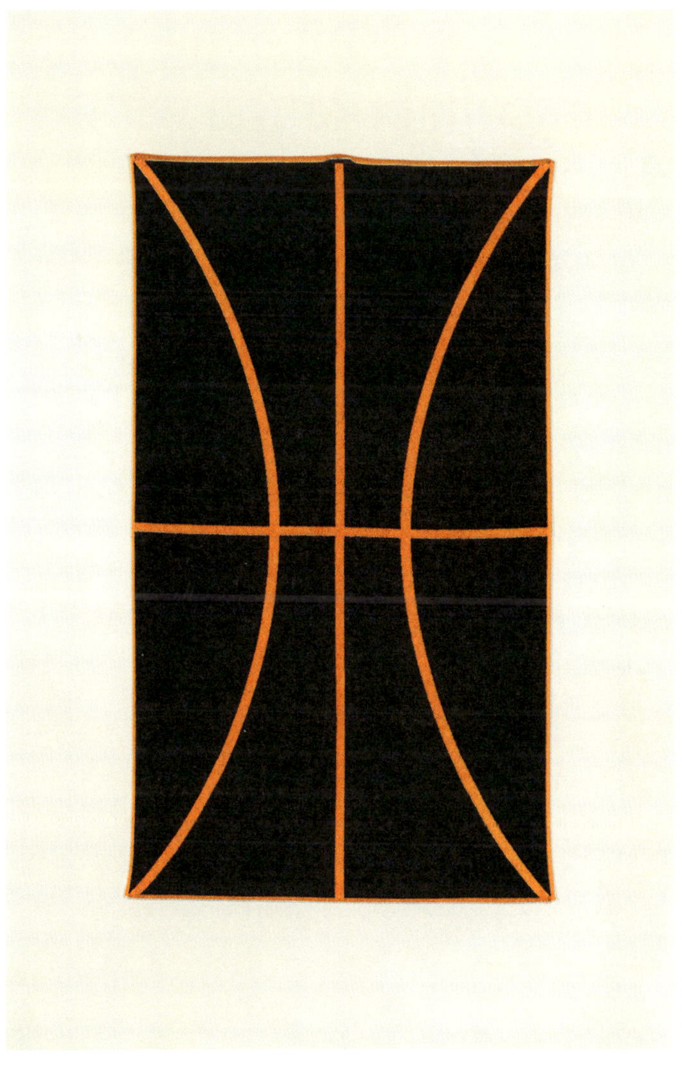

cat. 04

Arin Rungjang in collaboration with Guillaume Bijl *Melancholic Sense of Distance*

Where did it all begin? It is said "When Imana created this land, he grew so fond of it, he returned every night to rest." When did paradise become hell? From the start even the conquest was regrettable misunderstanding. Europe gave the land to its conqueror, and the king knew nothing of it. It was never about civilization, never about tribe or race. It was always about greed, arrogance and power. And when finally grasped the horror, it was too late. From Kibuye in the West to Kibungo in the East, people gathered seeking refuge in churches by the thousands, in hospitals and schools. And when they were found, the old and the sick, women and children alike, they were killed. These killings were not spontaneous or accidental. It is not an African phenomenon and must never be viewed as such. We have seen it in industrialized Europe. We have seen it in Asia. We must have global vigilance and never again must we be shy in the face of the evidence. Yes, it's April again. Every year in April the rainy season starts. And every year, every day in April, a haunting emptiness descends over our hearts. Every year in April I remember how quickly life ends. Every year I remember how lucky I should feel to be alive. Every year in April, I remember.

Augustine

stamp, 50 euro note, ink

77 mm × 133 mm

2012

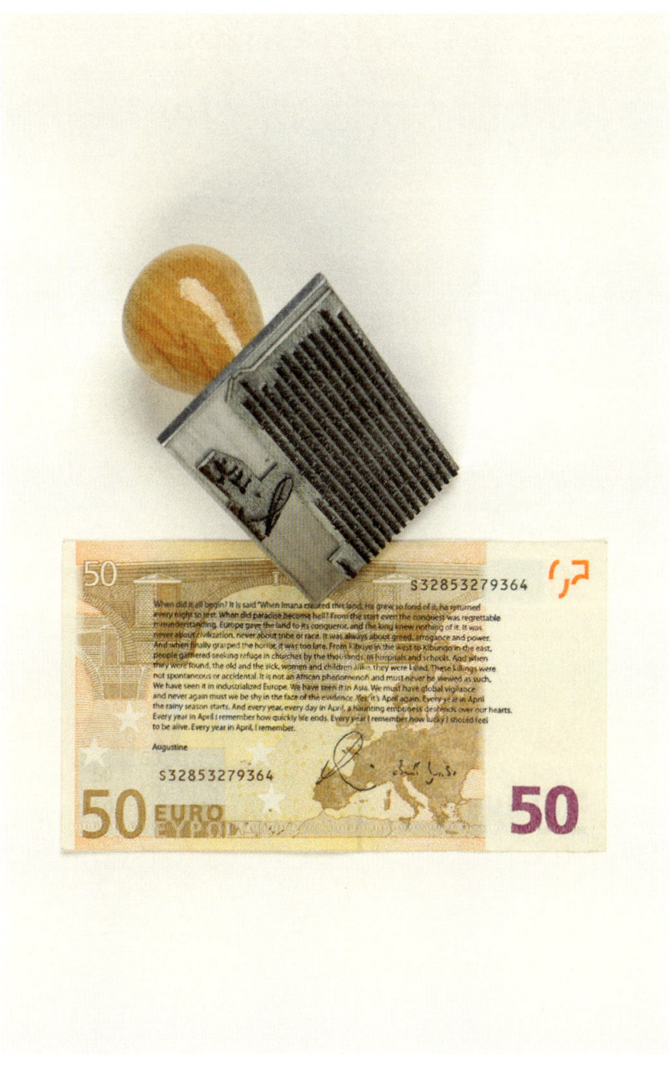
50
S32853279364
When did it all begin? It is said "When Imana created this land, He grew so fond of it, he returned
every night to rest. When did paradise become hell? From the start even the conquest was regrettable
misunderstanding. Europe gave the land to its conqueror, and the king knew nothing of it. It was
never about civilization, never about tribe or race. It was always about greed, arrogance and power.
And when finally grasped the horror, it was too late. From Kibuye in the west to Kibungo in the east,
people gathered seeking refuge in churches by the thousands, in hospitals and schools. And when
they were found, the old and the sick, women and children alike, they were killed. These killings were
not spontaneous or accidental. It is not an African phenomenon and must never be viewed as such.
We have seen it in industrialized Europe. We have seen it in Asia. We must have global vigilance
and never again must we be shy in the face of the evidence. Yes, it's April again. Every year in April
the rainy season starts. And every year, every day in April, a haunting emptiness descends over our hearts.
Every year in April I remember how quickly life ends. Every year I remember how lucky I should feel
to be alive. Every year in April, I remember.
Augustine
S32853279364
50 EURO
50

cat. 05

Ella de Burca
Fin (I'm Still Here)

black paint
Ø 20 mm
2012

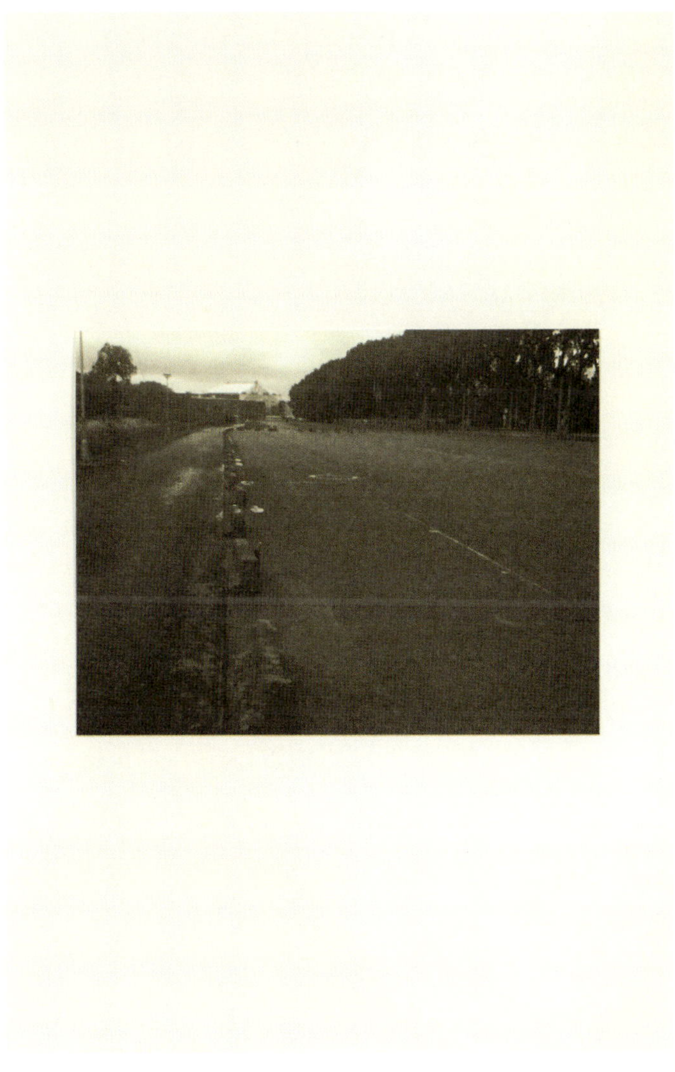

cat. 06

Ryan Siegan-Smith

grey relief paint
50 mm × 20 mm
2012

SINT - PAULUS
STELLA ARTOIS
AMBERES
STELLA ARTOIS
Coca-Cola zero
zero
10

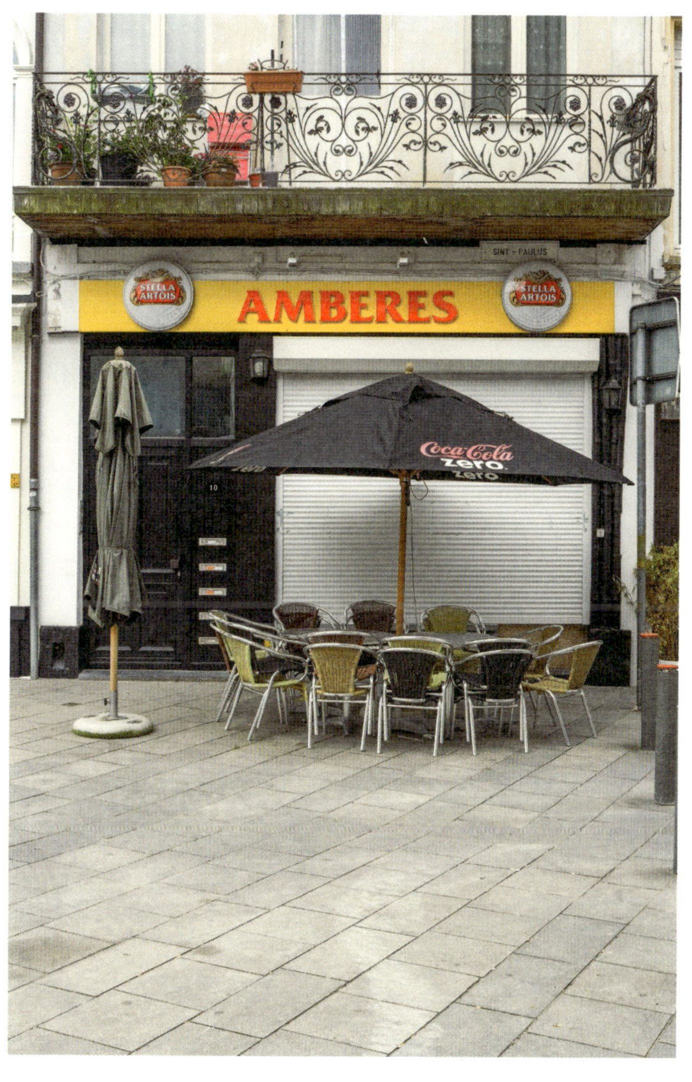

cat. 07

André Romão

xerox print
297 mm × 210 mm
2012

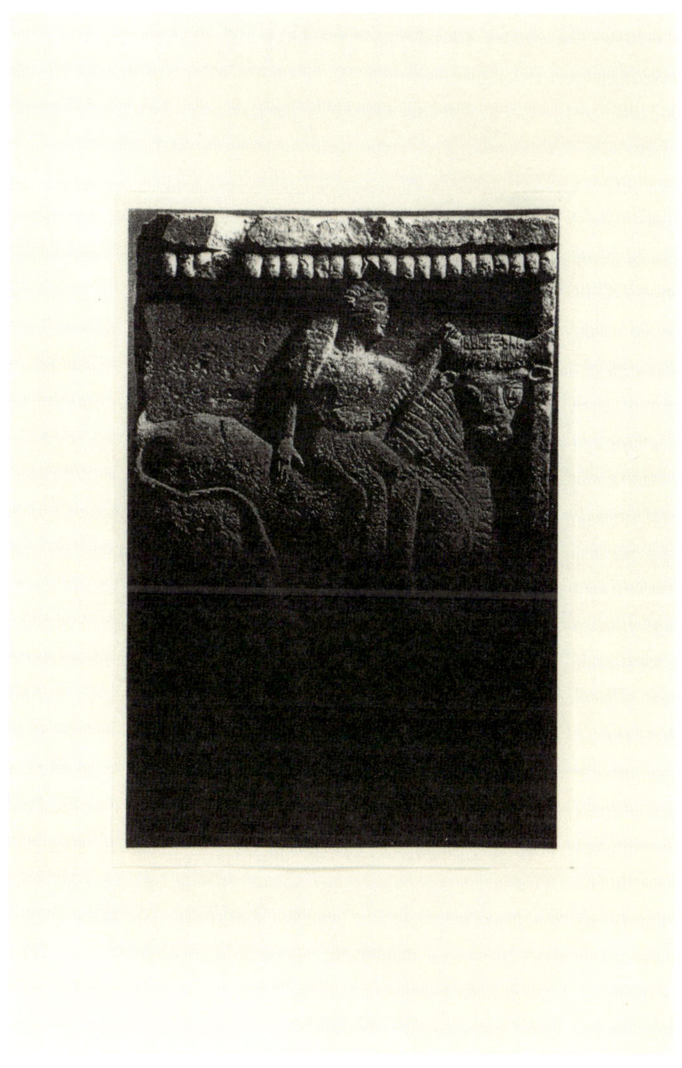

cat. 08

Mounira Al Solh
Agenda

cardboard, ink
600 mm × 800 mm
2012

cat. 09

Francesc Ruiz
Salami Love

copied fragment out of a comic by Rolando Del Fico
291 mm × 210 mm
2012

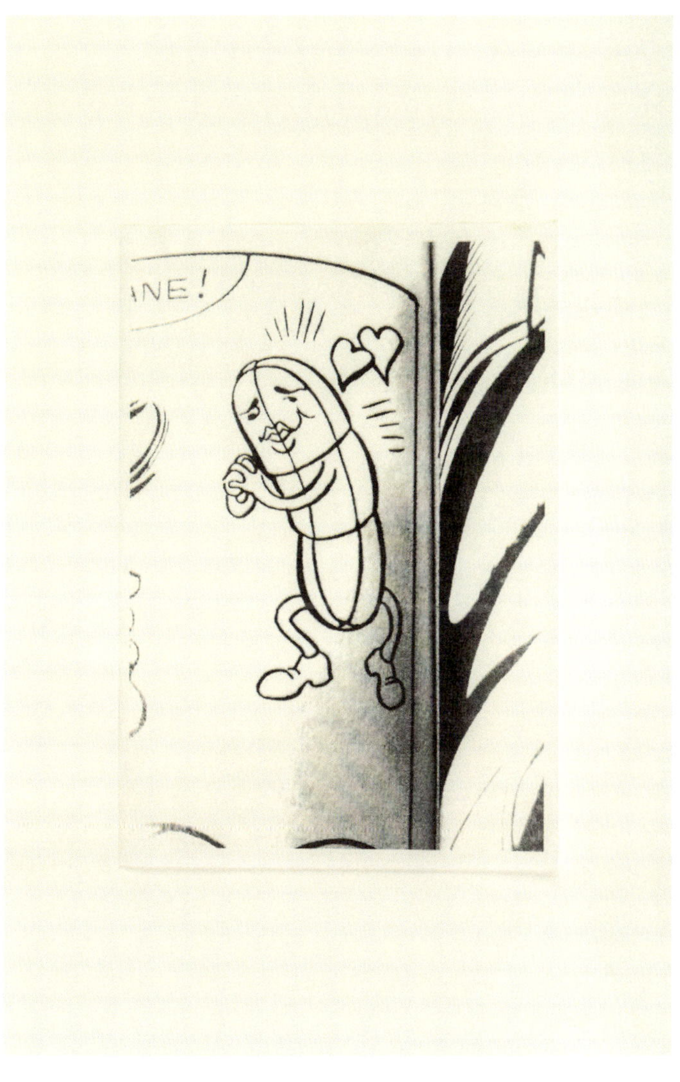

cat. 10

Pedro Barateiro
Heritage

6 modified prints of tapestries, black paint
375 mm × 310 mm
2013

cat. 11

Philip Janssens
Tuning

2 posters, black frame
51 mm × 41 mm
2013

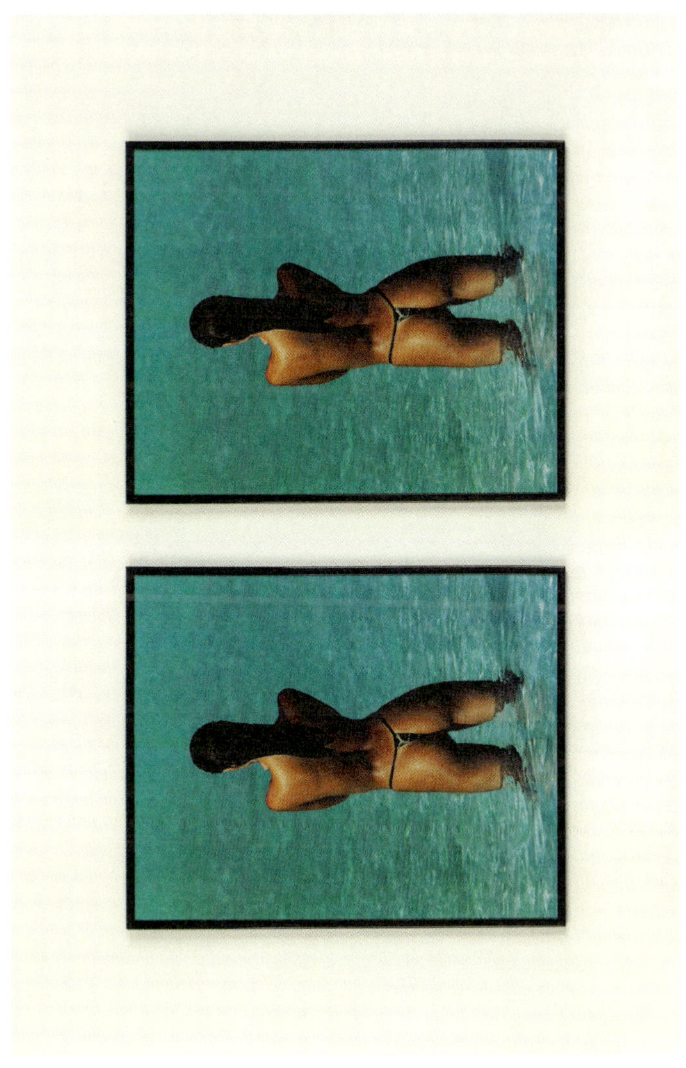

cat. 12

Darren Roshier

De Antwerpse hou niet van om Frans te spreken

framed A4 sized paper, pencil
297 mm × 210 mm
2013

HEBBEN - TO HAVE
IK HEB
JE HEBT
U HEBT
HIJ HEEFT
ZE HEEFT
HET HEEFT
WE HEBBEN
JULLIE HEBBEN
ZE HEBBEN
ZIJN - TO BE
IK BEN
JE BENT
U BENT
HIJ IS
ZE IS
HET IS
WE ZIJN
JULLIE ZIJN
ZE ZIJN
GAAN - TO GO
IK GA
JE GAAT
U GAAT
HIJ GAAT
ZE GAAT
HET GAAT
WE GAAN
JULLIE GAAN
ZE GAAN
ZULLEN (KOMEN) - WILL (COME)
IK ZAL KOMEN
JE ZULT/ZAL KOMEN
U ZULT/ZAL KOMEN
HIJ ZAL KOMEN
ZE ZAL KOMEN
HET ZAL KOMEN
WE ZULLEN KOMEN
JULLIE ZULLEN KOMEN
ZE ZULLEN KOMEN
KUNNEN - TO BE ABLE TO
IK KAN
JE KUNT/KAN
U KUNT/KAN
HIJ KAN
ZE KAN
HET KAN
WE KUNNEN
JULLIE KUNNEN
ZE KUNNEN
WILLEN - TO WANT
IK WIL
JE WIL/WILT
U WILT
HIJ WIL
ZE WIL
HET WIL
WE WILLEN
JULLIE WILLEN
ZE WILLEN
MOGEN - TO BE ABLE TO - PERMISSION
IK MAG
JE MAG
U MAG
HIJ MAG
ZE MAG
HET MAG
WE MOGEN
JULLIE MOGEN
ZE MOGEN

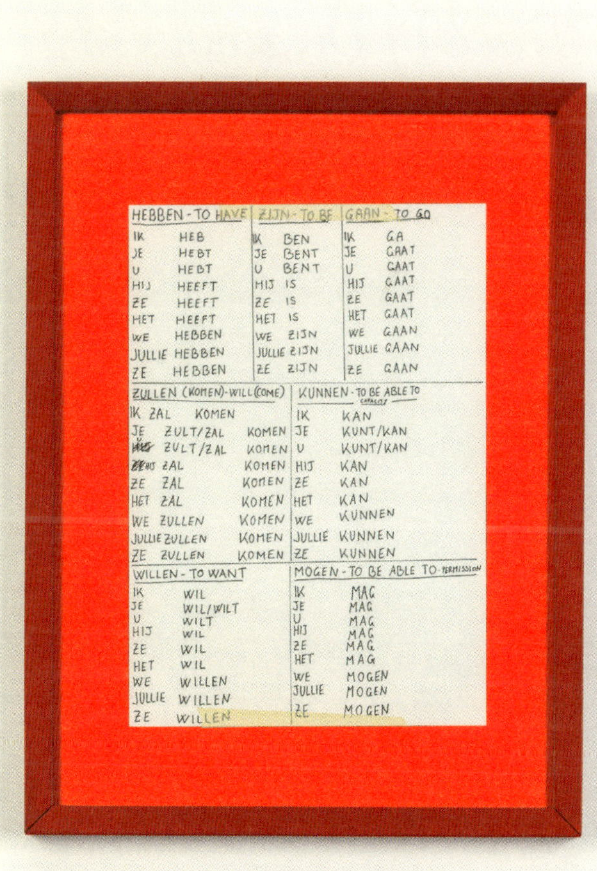

cat. 13

Ilaria Lupo
Trace of De Sokkel #5

clay, stone
287 mm × 100 mm
2013

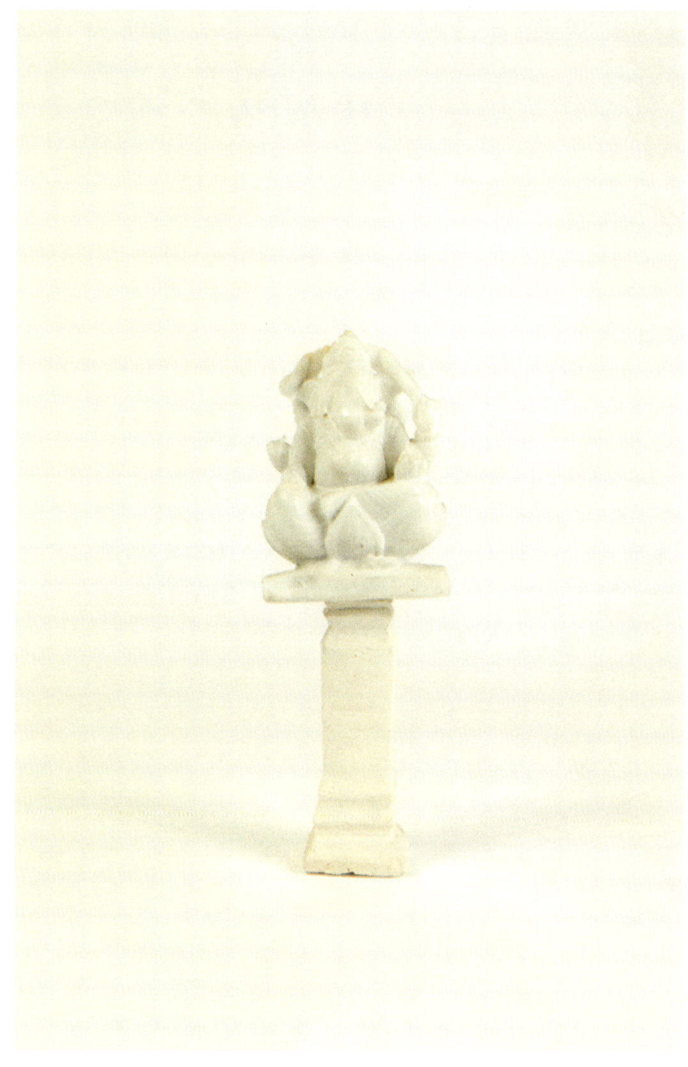

cat. 14

Naneci Yurdagül
Die Yurdagüls

glass bottle, paper, glue
300 mm × 100 mm
2013

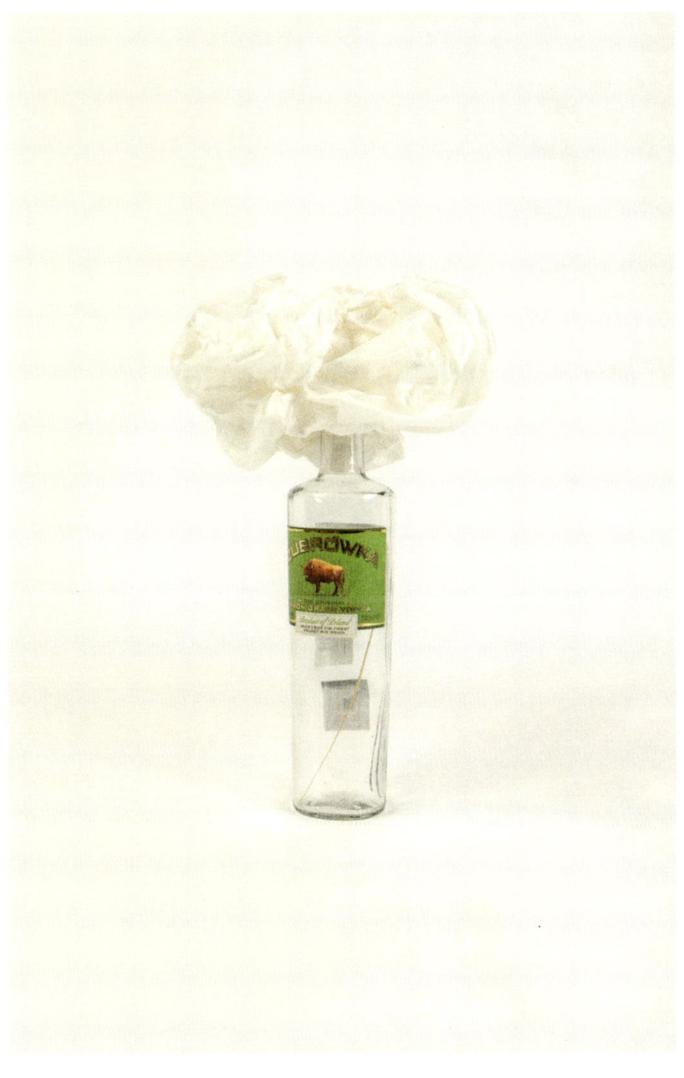

cat. 15

Post Brothers

plastic glasses
40 mm × 140 mm
2013

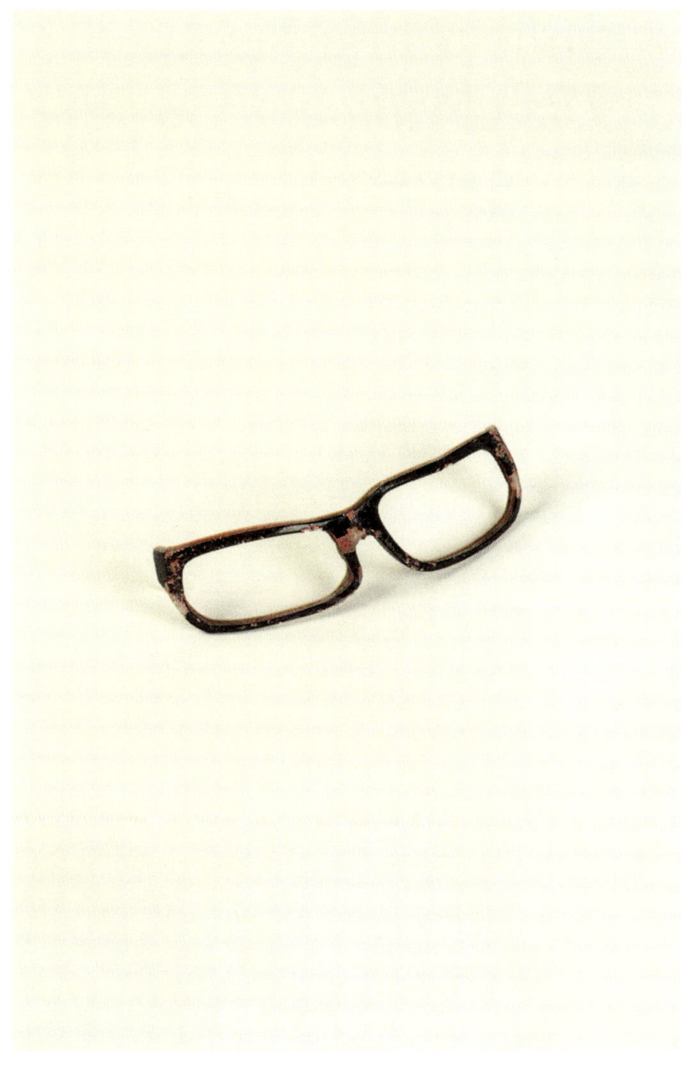

cat. 16

Stine Marie Jacobsen
The Creation of David Armstrong Six

nylon wig, head in styrofoam
300 mm × 210 mm
2013

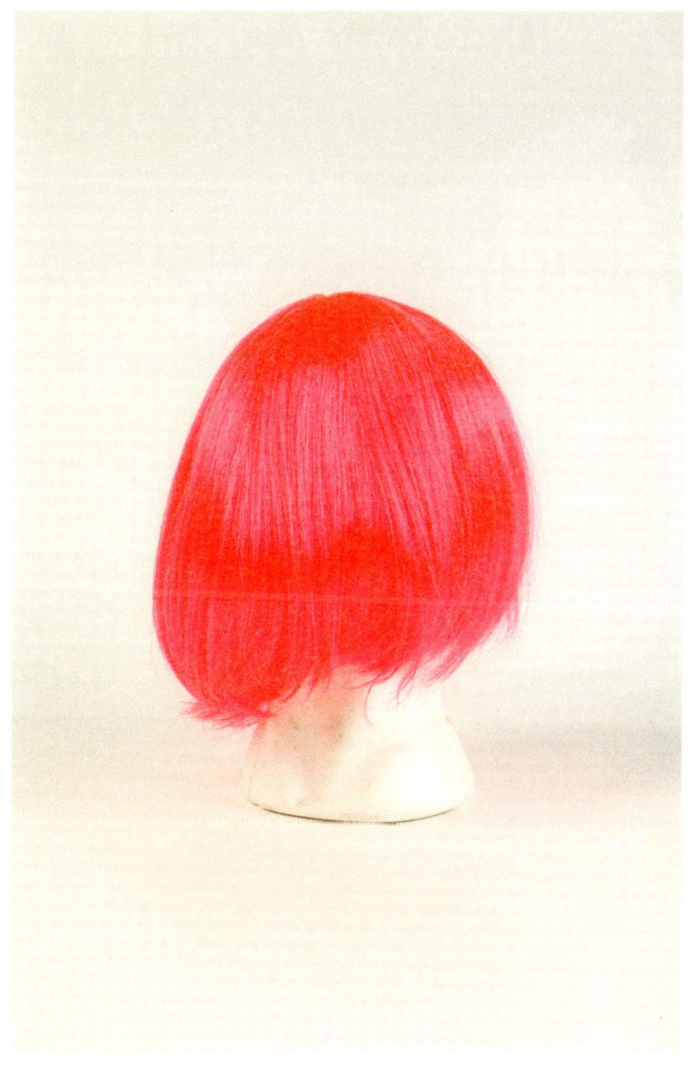

cat. 17

Bhagwati Prasad

cotton
240 mm × 100 mm
2013

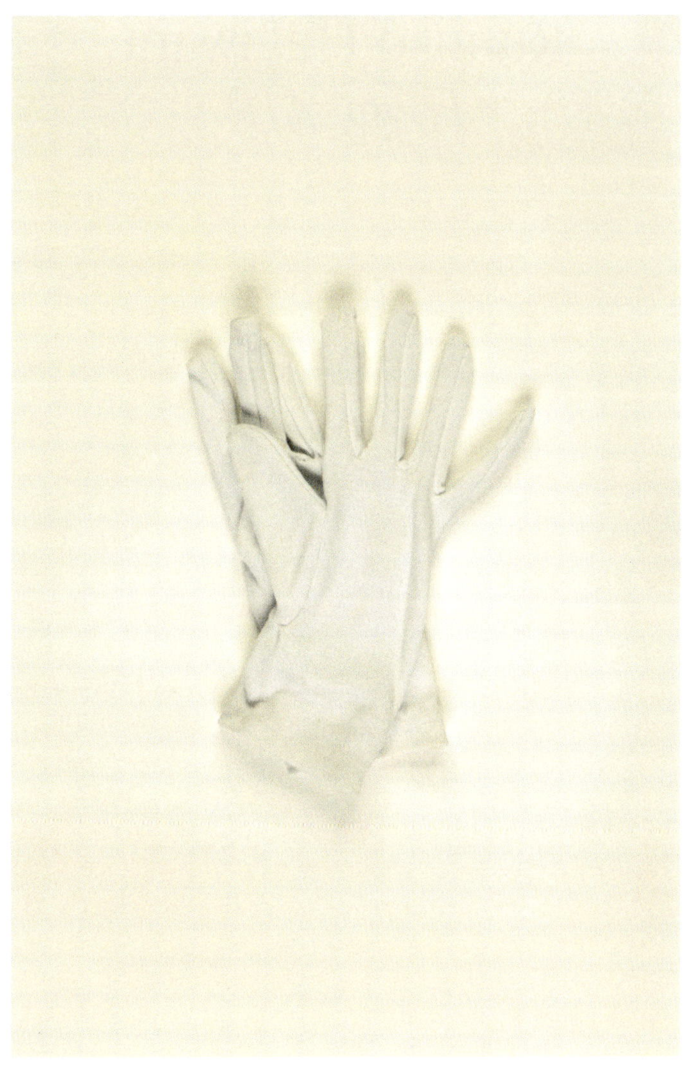

cat. 18

Rumiko Hagiwara
Foggy AIR

photoprint, frame and title plate

215 mm × 165 mm

2013

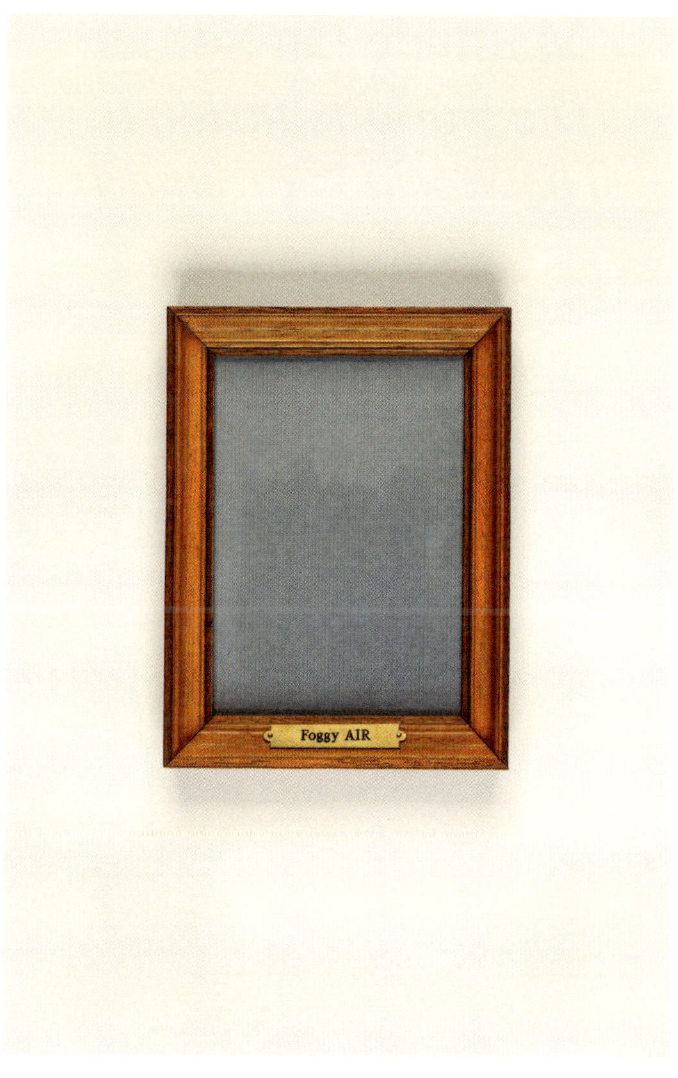

cat. 19

Mathilde Du Sordet
The world is inside It. The World is around It

publication
297 mm × 210 mm
2013

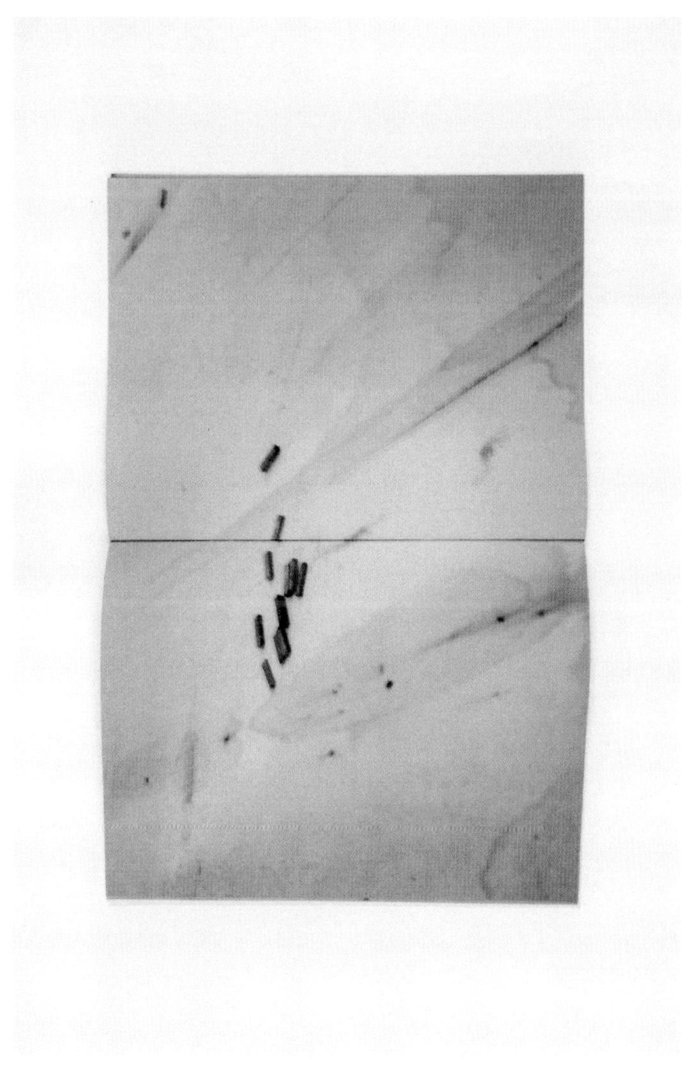

cat. 20

Harry Heirmans

foam rubber
Ø 50 mm
2013

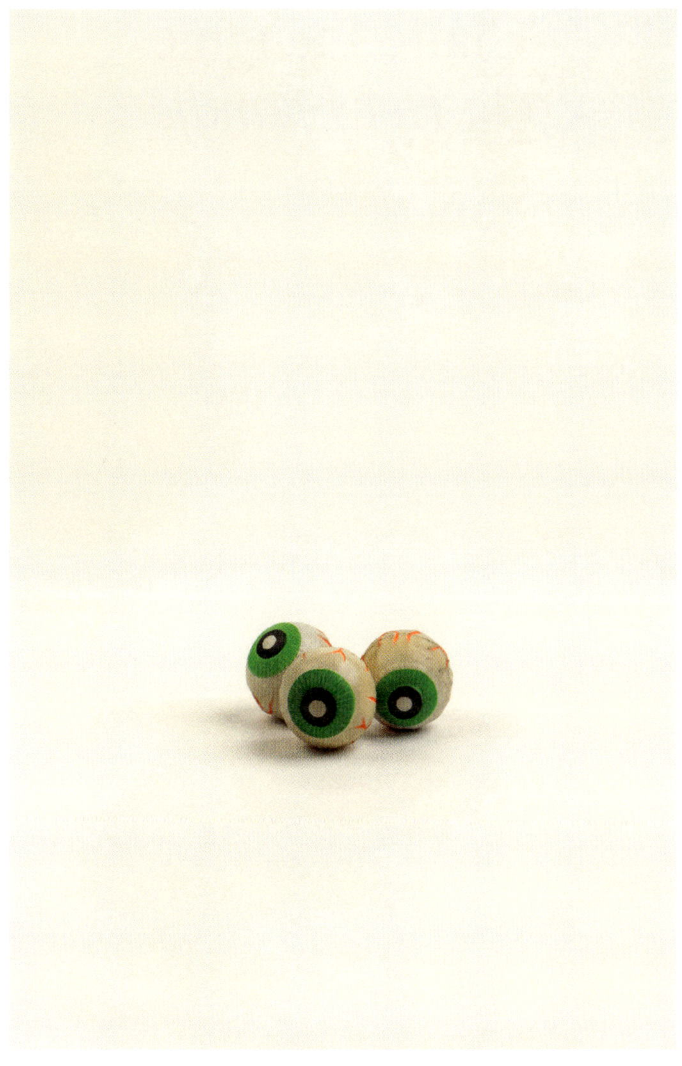

cat. 21

Claire Liengme
On Het Eilandje

envelop, paper
297 mm × 210 mm
2014

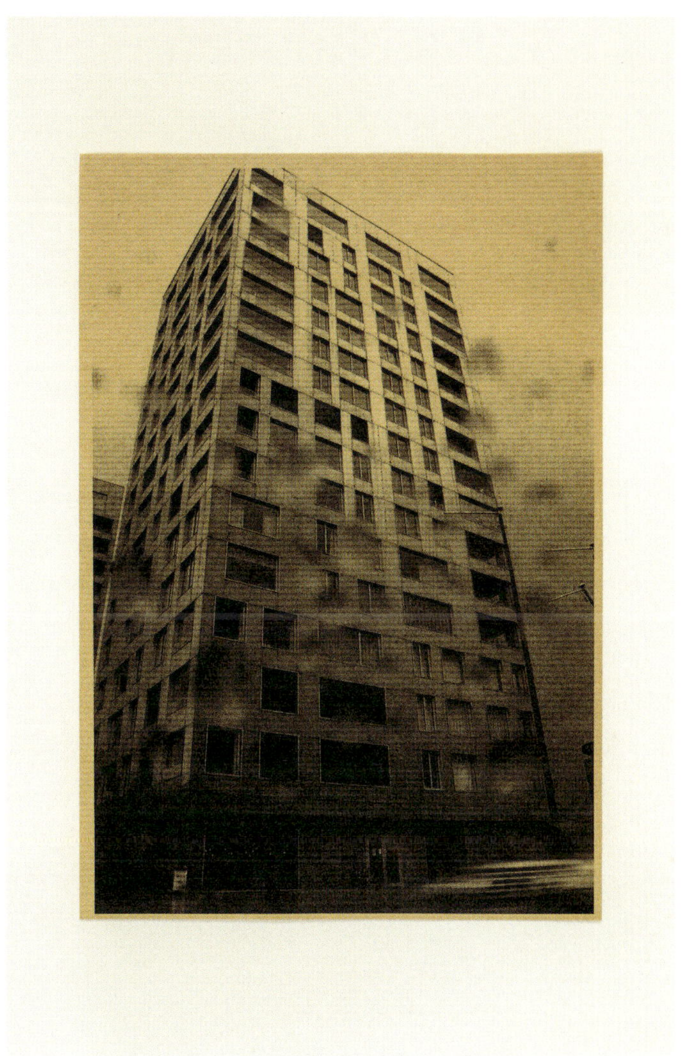

cat. 22

Fabian Rouwette

printed photo
482 mm × 330 mm
2014

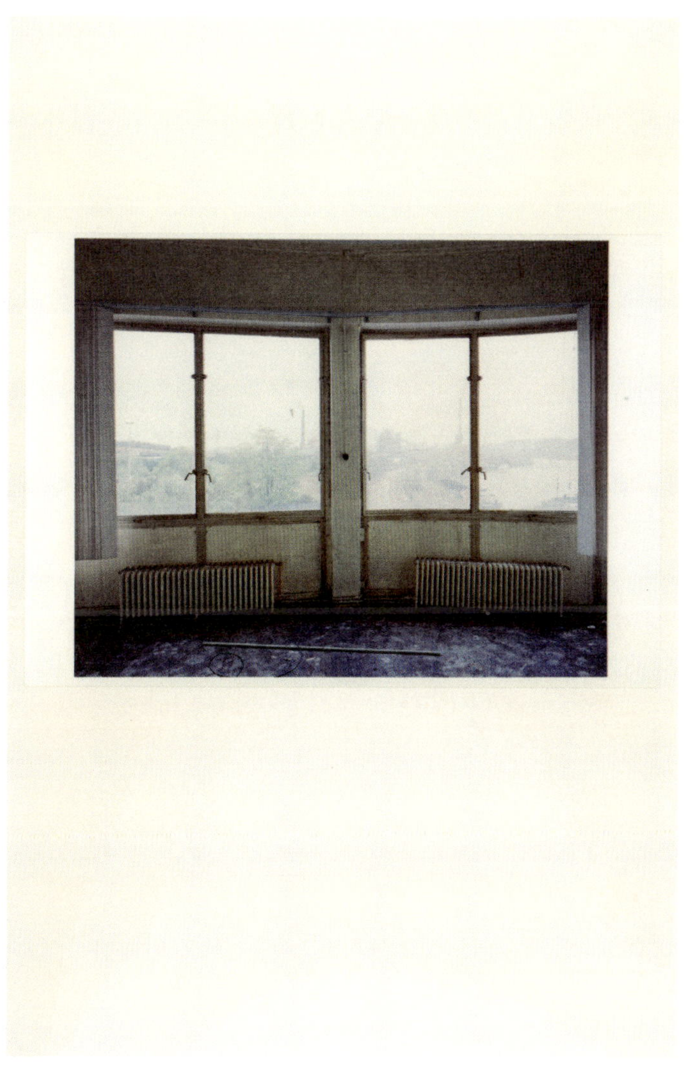

cat. 23

Antoine Van Impe
CKLOC

counterclockwise clock

Ø 250 mm

2014

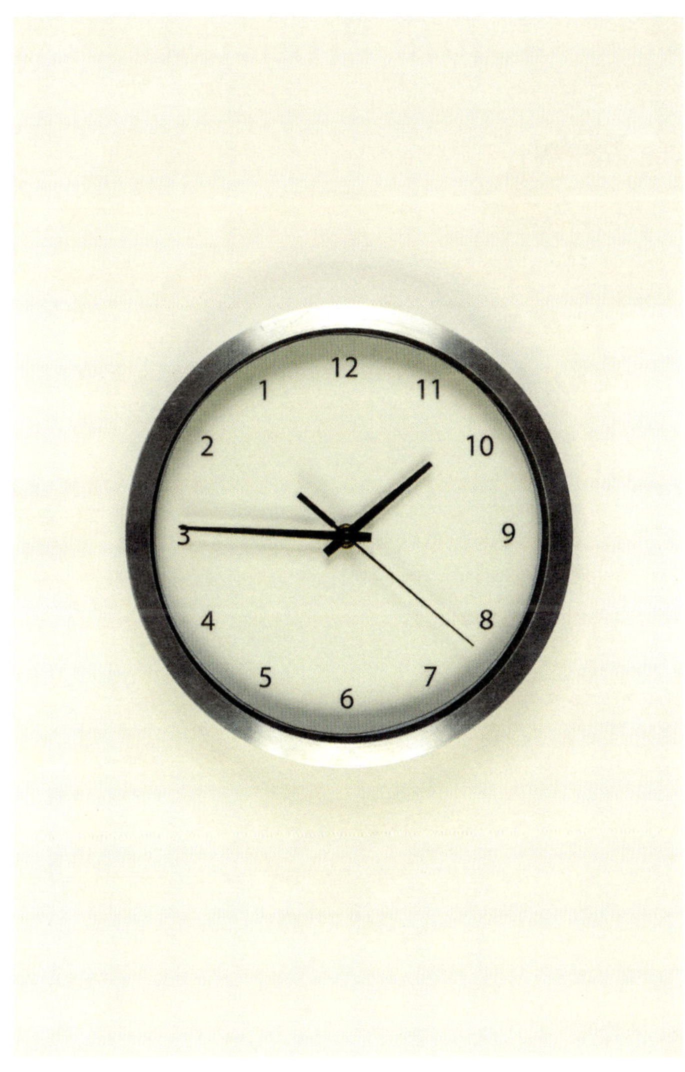

cat. 24

Laure Prouvost

bread, blue paint, plate
260 mm × 190 mm
2014

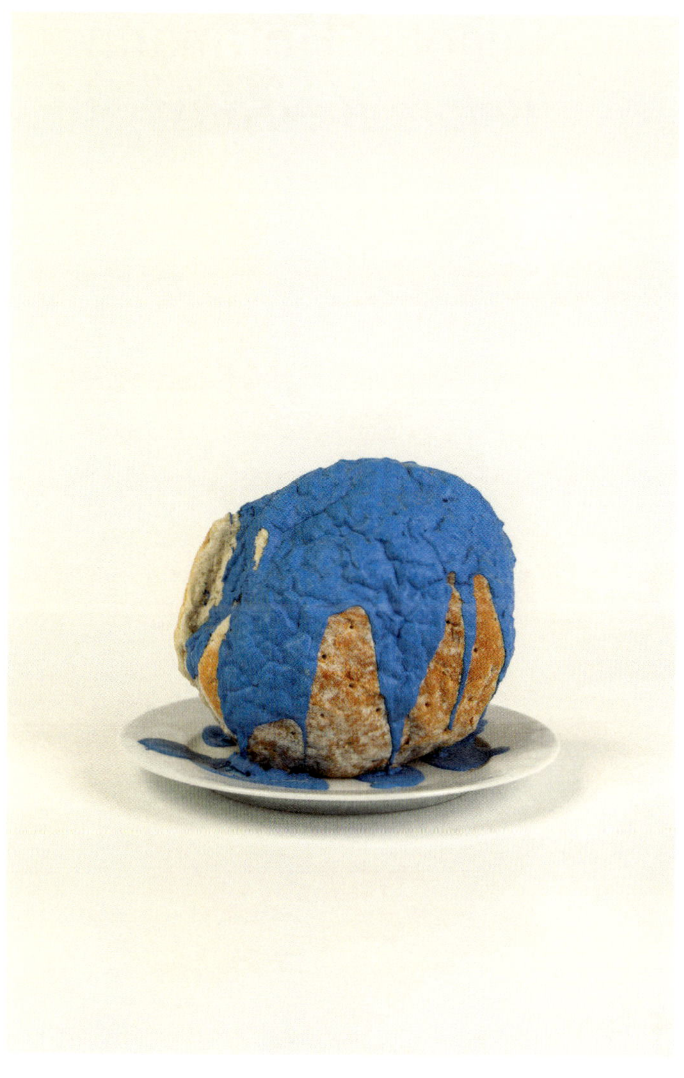

cat. 25

Nicholas Hoffman
Before Breakfast

door, Judas hole
dimensions variable
2014

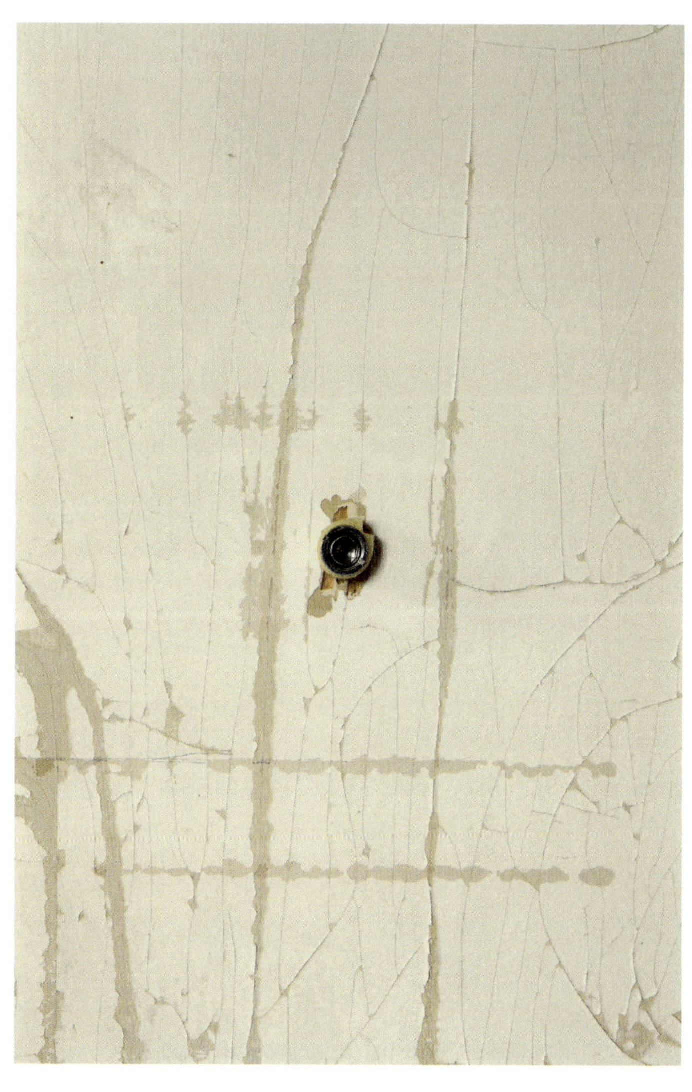

cat. 26

Savage
Simon

synthetic hairdresser training head, trimmed
180 mm × 300 mm
2014

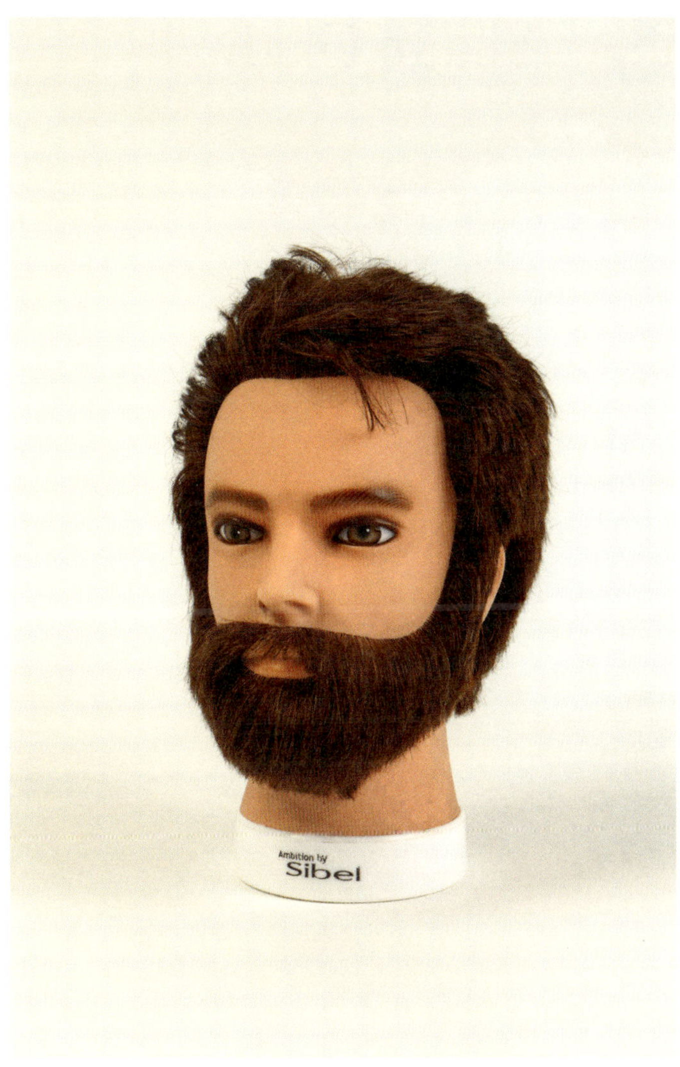

cat. 27

Shaun Gladwell

aluminium plate, aerosol
298 mm × 298 mm
2014

cat. 28

Dennis Tyfus

Ultra Eczema's Faeskroketten

sticker

300 mm × 400 mm

2014

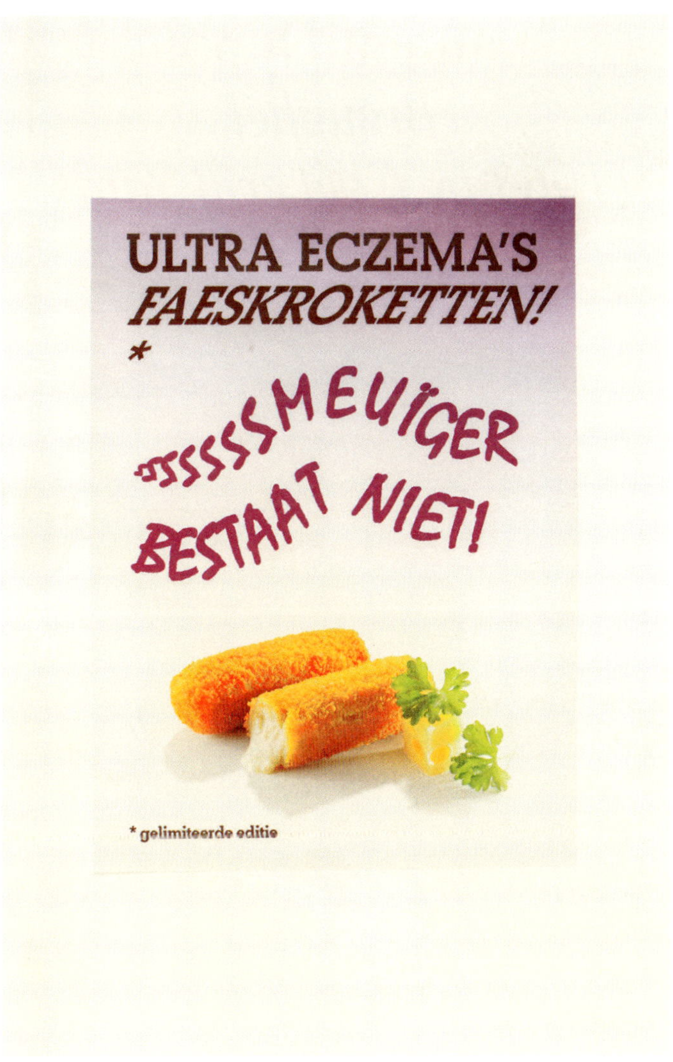
ULTRA ECZEMA'S
FAESKROKETTEN!
*
SSSSSSMEUïGER
BESTAAT NIET!
* gelimiteerde editie

cat. 29

Laurent Dupont
Breughel (1963 by Cockerill Yards, Hoboken)

print and oil on canvas, paper
483 mm × 329 mm
2014

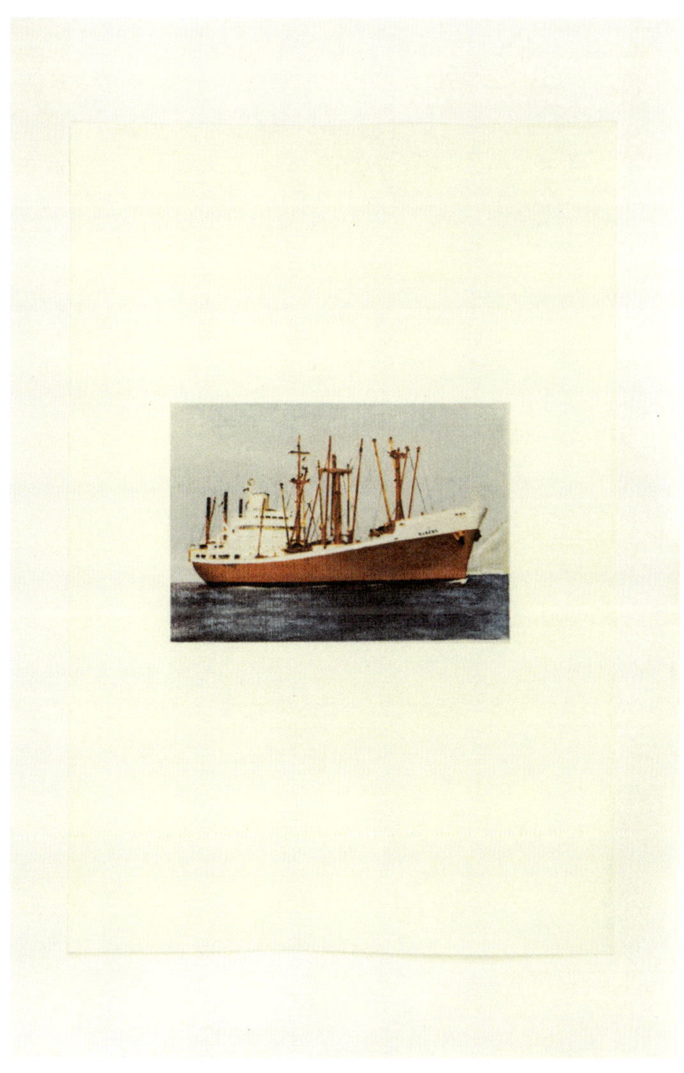

cat. 30

Simon Feydieu
Untitled

shoes, overall, T-shirt
300 mm × 350 mm
2015

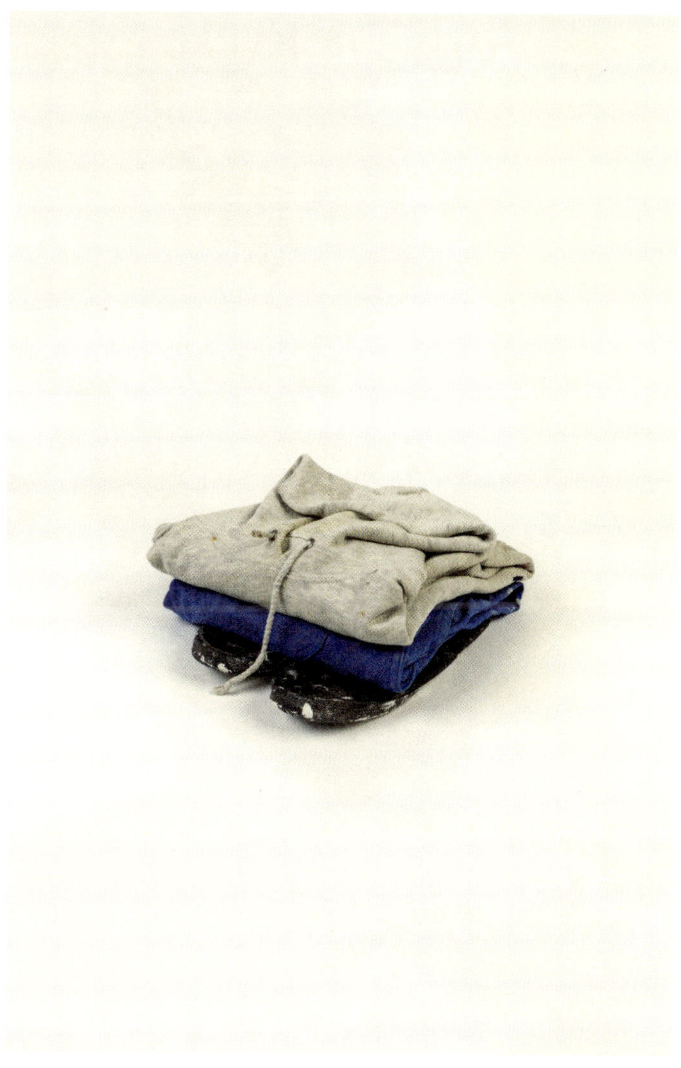

cat. 31

Joris De Rycke

8 diaframes, pelicule
50 mm × 50 mm
2015

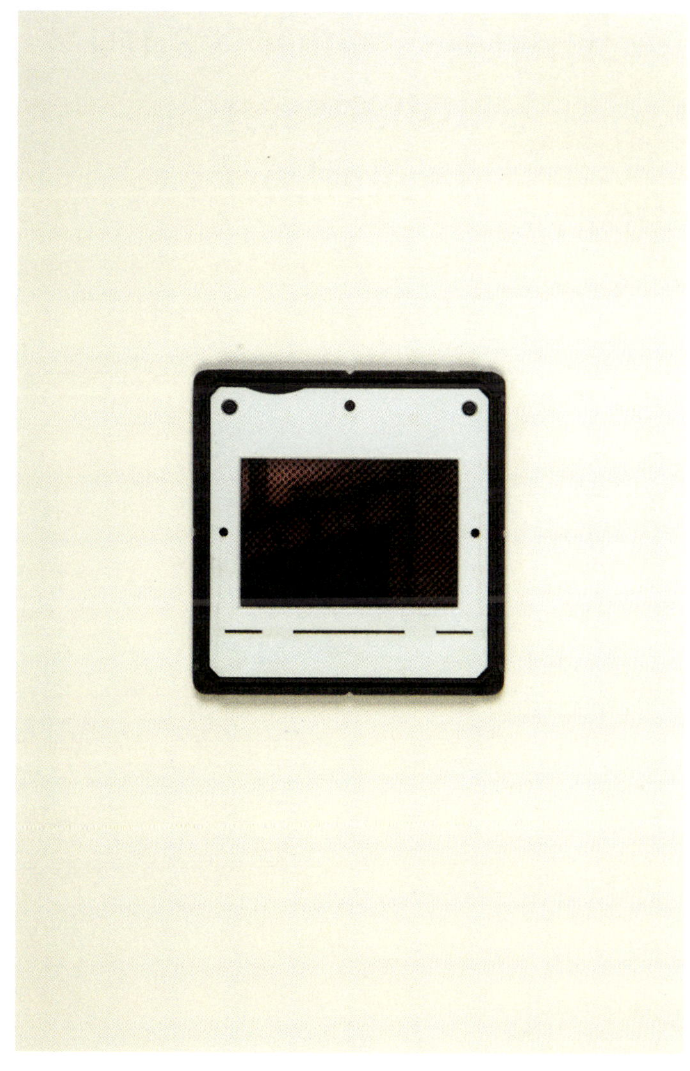

cat. 32

Rasmus Søndergaard Johanssen
Stirring Sticks

offcuts, extracted resin, coal dust, pressed wood plate
594 mm × 611 mm
2015

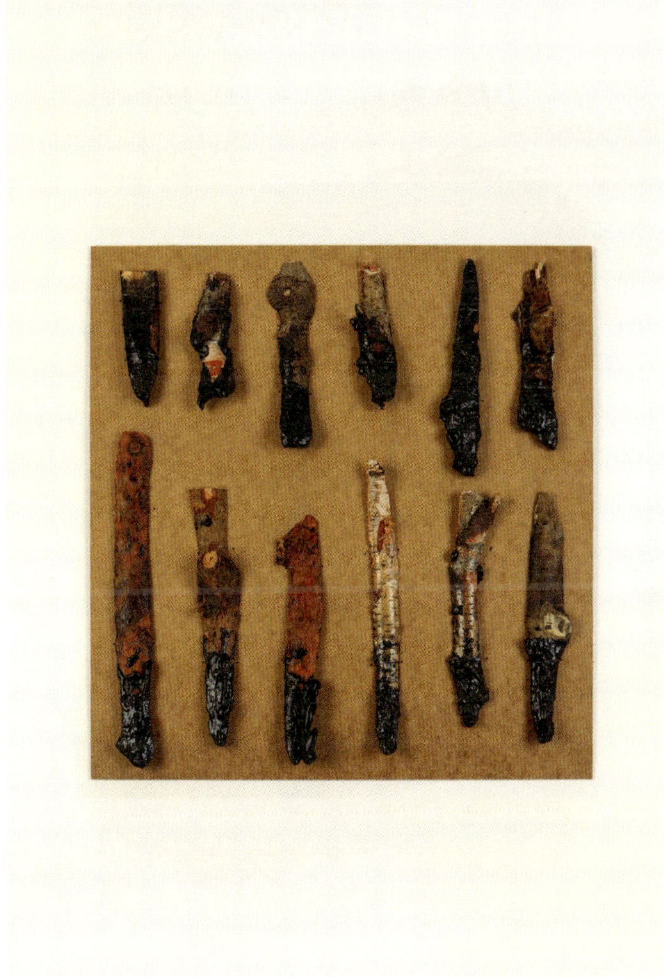

cat. 33

Yan Tomaszewski
The Boogeyman

chocolate finger
60 mm × 150 mm
2015

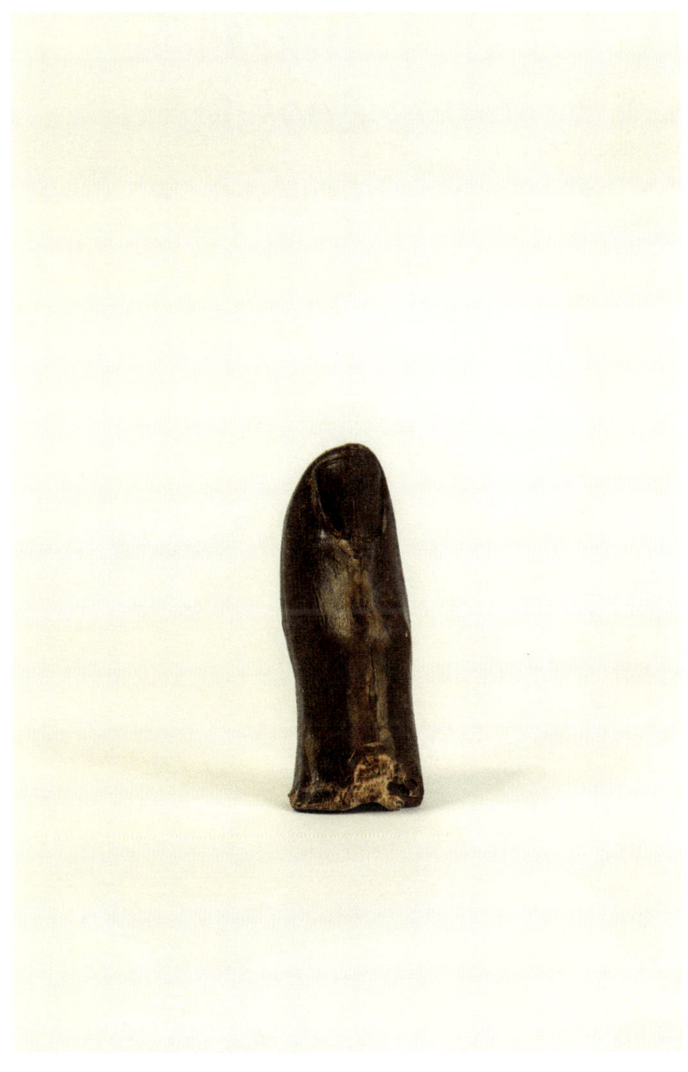

cat. 34

Serra Tansel
Good Looking

nazar sticker, protection against the evil eye,
on the peephole of the bedroom door
20 mm × 20 mm
2015

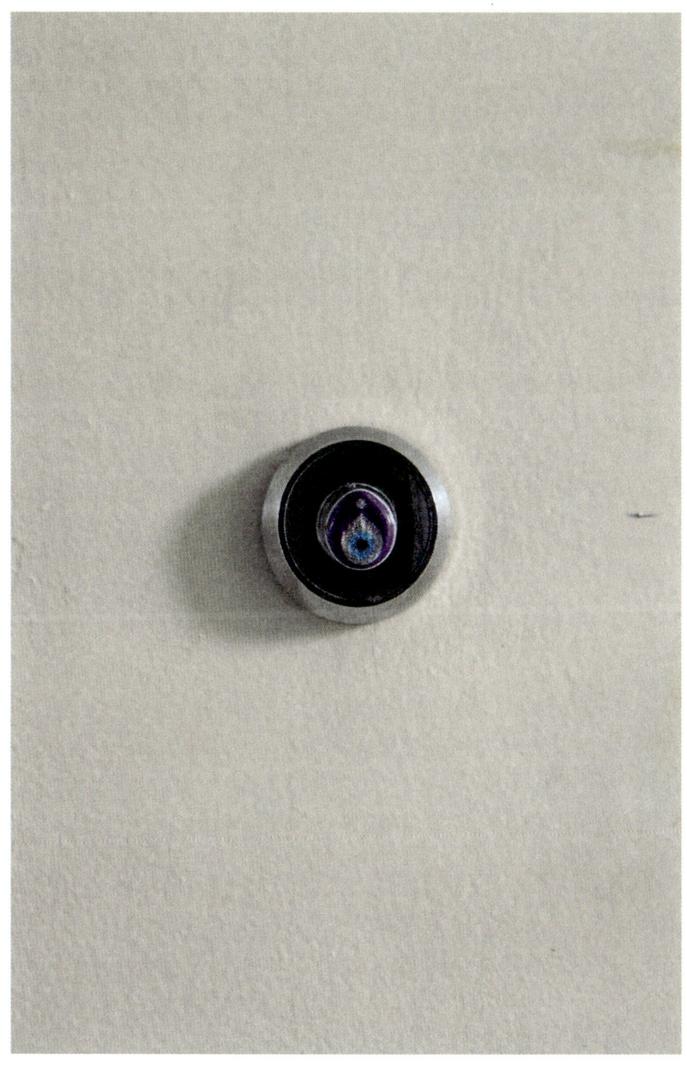

cat. 35

Baptiste Croze
MAN_VROUW

2 blue back posters
1189 mm × 841 mm
2015

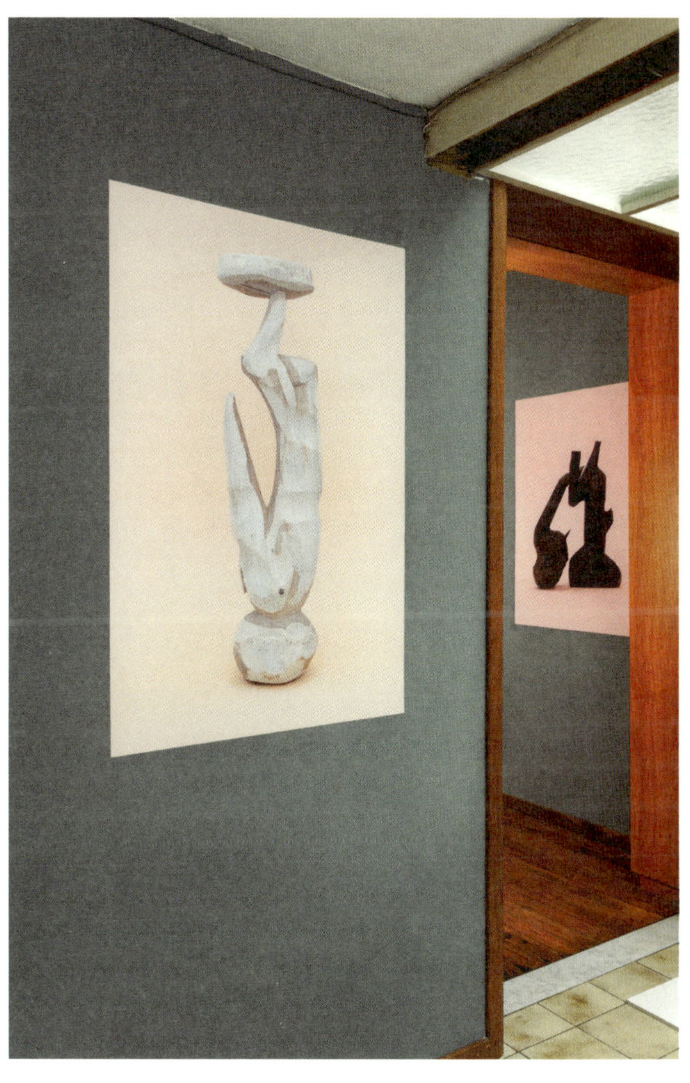

cat. 36

Mike Cooper

text on paper
420 mm × 297 mm
2015

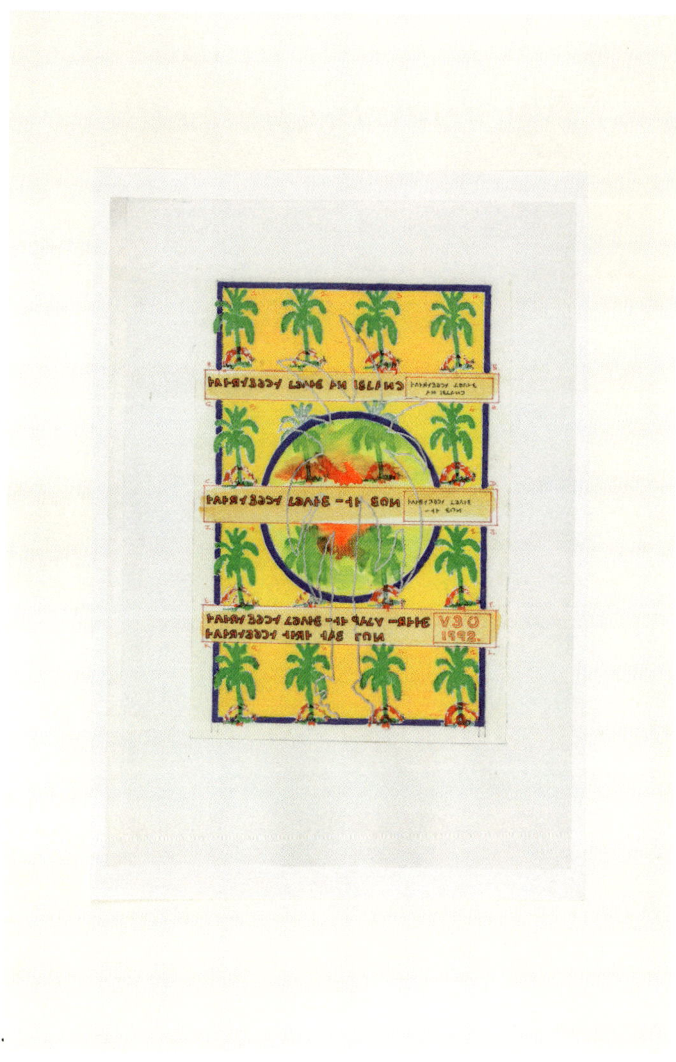

cat. 37

Reg Carremans
Typology bottle / can

plastic, tin, paper
dimensions variable
2014

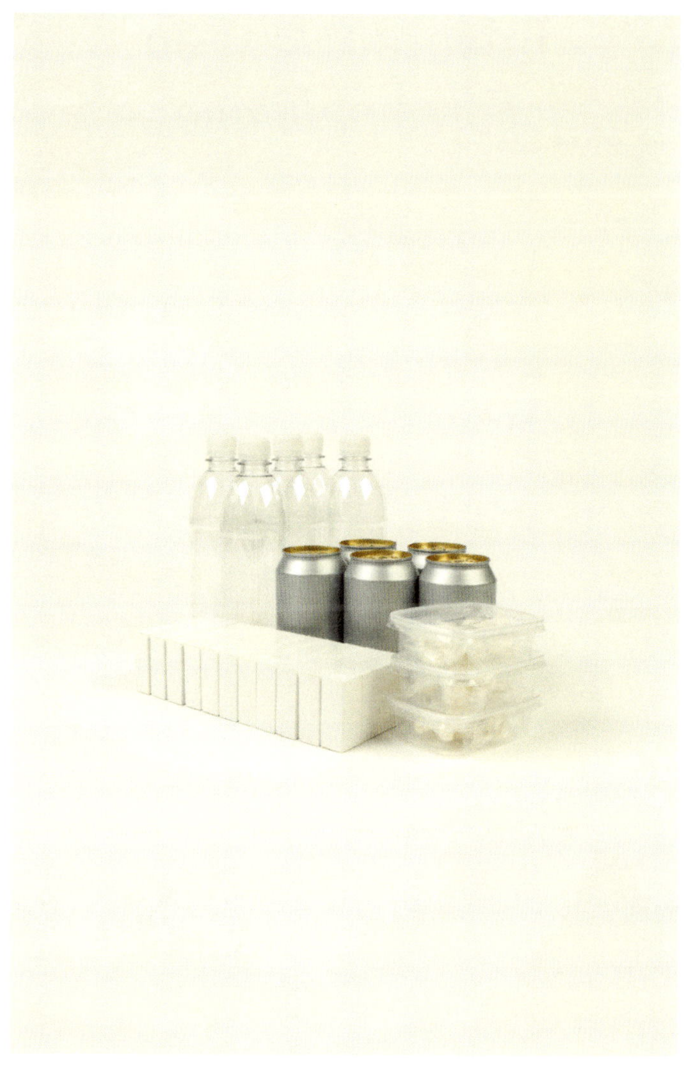

cat. 38

Edgardo Aragón
Force publique

photograph
210 mm × 144 mm
2015

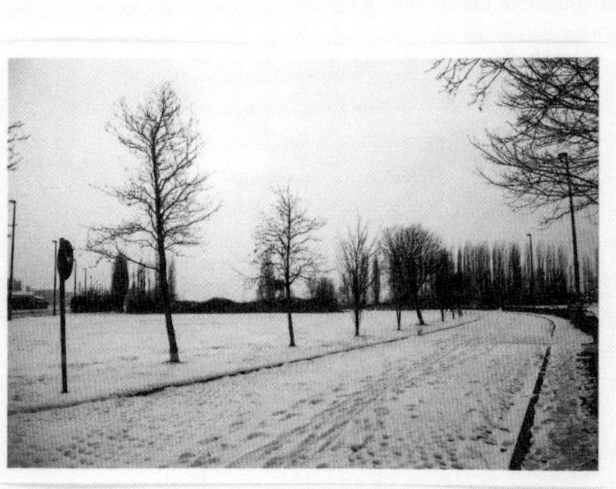

cat. 39

Bianca Baldi
Tot tibi sunt dotes Virgo quot sidera caelo

script
220 mm × 340 mm
2016

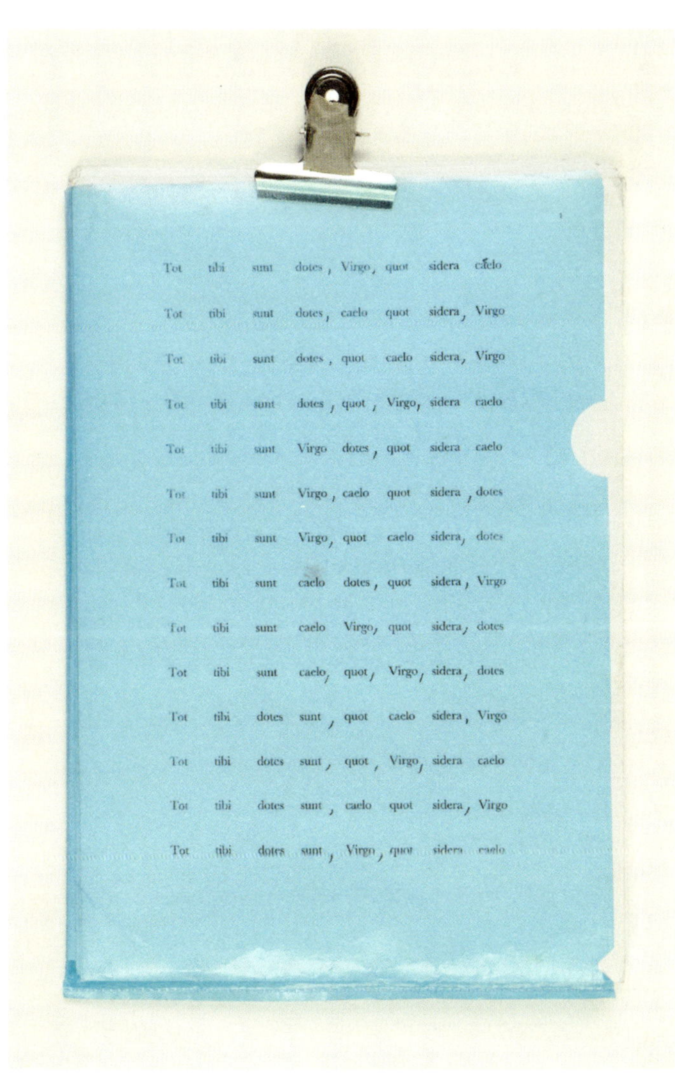
Tot tibi sunt dotes, Virgo, quot sidera caelo
Tot tibi sunt dotes, caelo quot sidera, Virgo
Tot tibi sunt dotes, quot caelo sidera, Virgo
Tot tibi sunt dotes, quot, Virgo, sidera caelo
Tot tibi sunt Virgo dotes, quot sidera caelo
Tot tibi sunt Virgo, caelo quot sidera, dotes
Tot tibi sunt Virgo, quot caelo sidera, dotes
Tot tibi sunt caelo dotes, quot sidera, Virgo
Tot tibi sunt caelo Virgo, quot sidera, dotes
Tot tibi sunt caelo, quot, Virgo, sidera, dotes
Tot tibi dotes sunt, quot caelo sidera, Virgo
Tot tibi dotes sunt, quot, Virgo, sidera caelo
Tot tibi dotes sunt, caelo quot sidera, Virgo
Tot tibi dotes sunt, Virgo, quot sidera caelo

cat. 40

Victoria Wigzell

scrabble stones
188 mm × 132 mm
2016

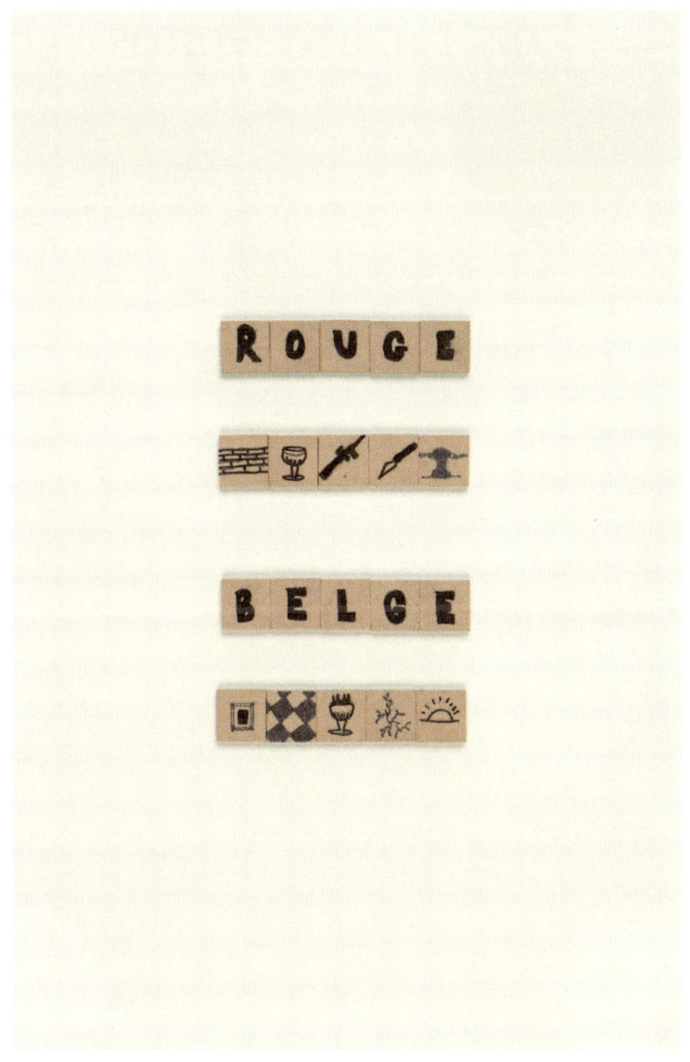

cat. 41

Luis Lázaro Matos

plastic, paper, color markers
1000 mm × 200 mm
2016

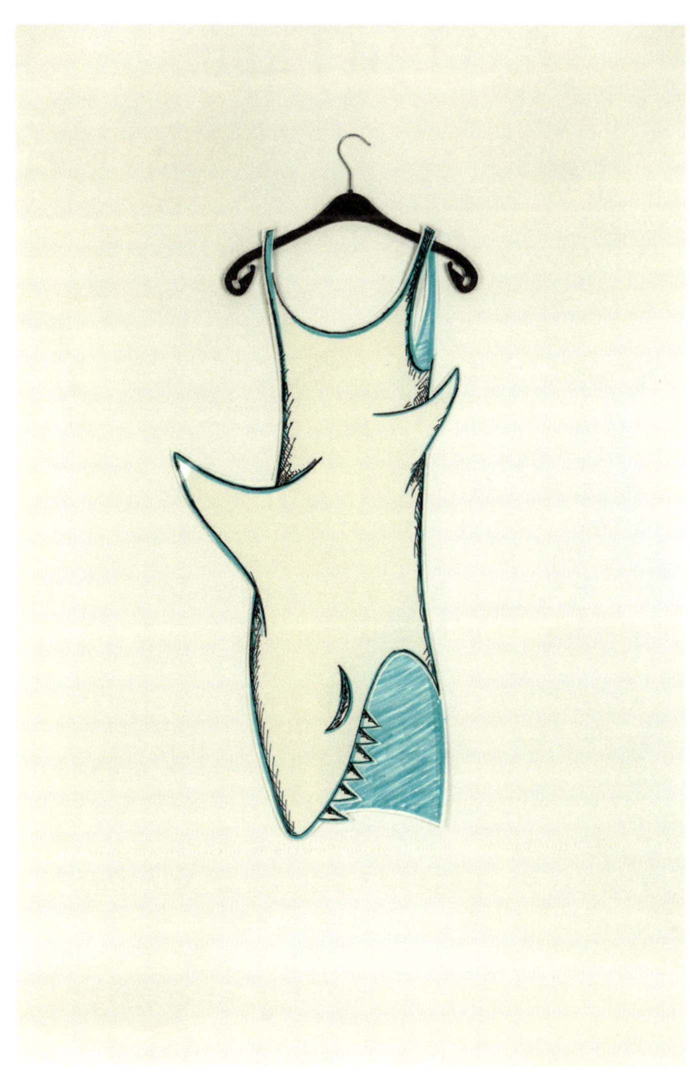

cat. 42

Lennart Lahuis

glass beads, paper, glue
50 mm × 100 mm
2016

cat. 43

Lodewijk Heylen

concrete
300 mm × 10 mm × 20 mm
2016

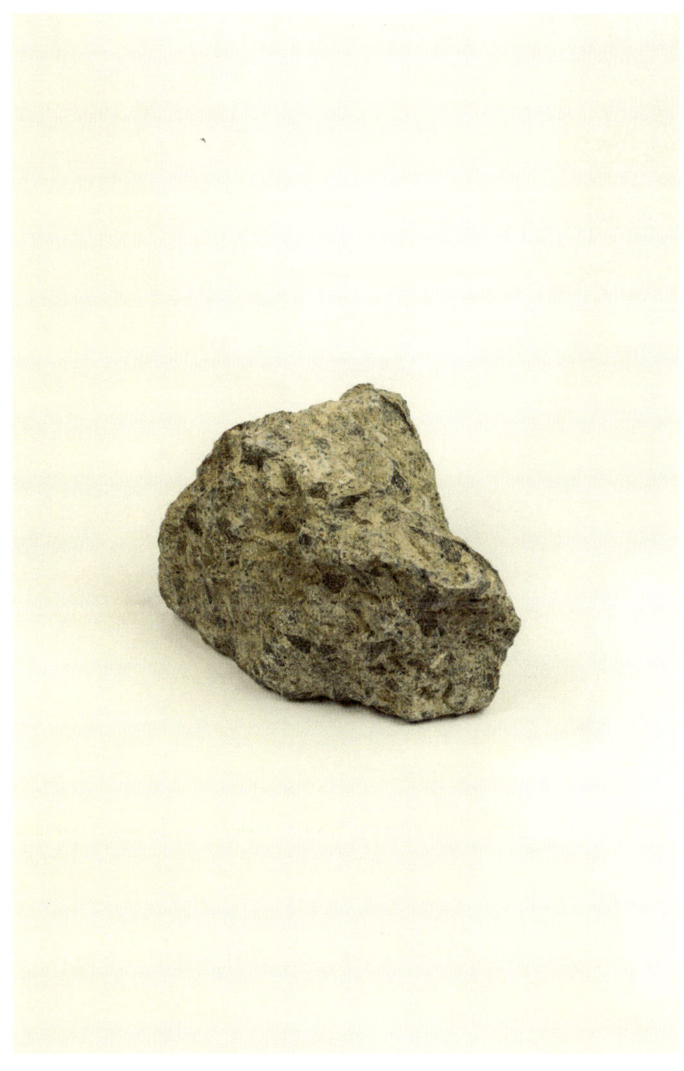

cat. 44

Alberto García del Castillo
Retrospective

reading copy, offset print on paper
110 mm × 180 mm
2016

RETROSPECTIVE
ALBERTO GARCÍA DEL CASTILLO
SHELTER PRESS — SP062

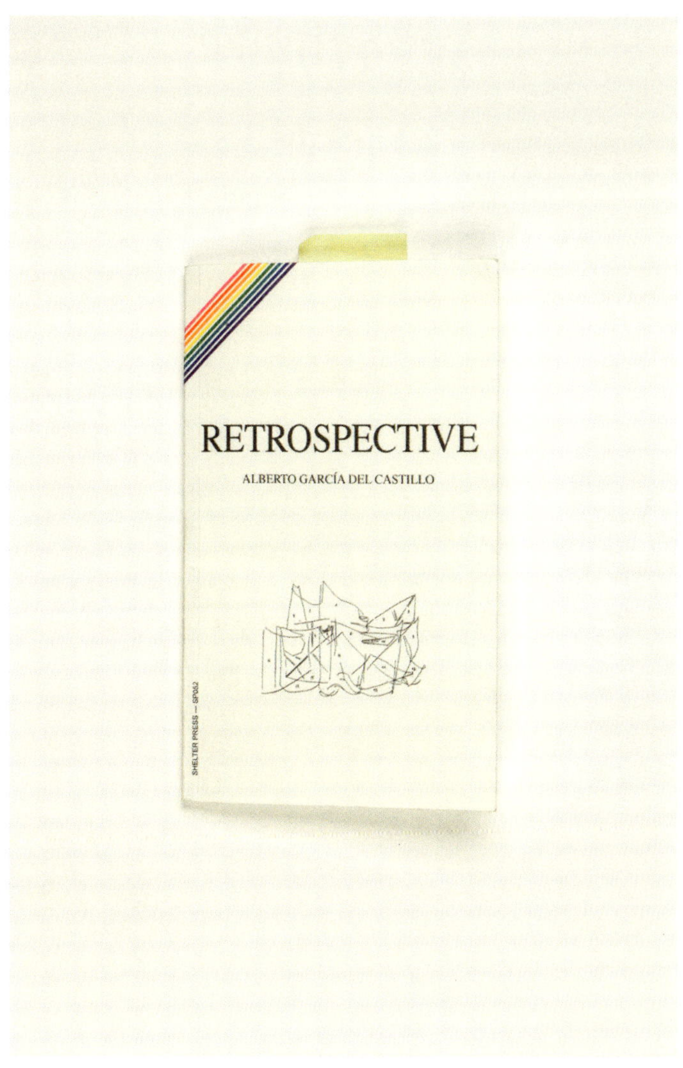

cat. 45

Ani Schulze

paper, plastic
841 mm × 1189 mm
2016

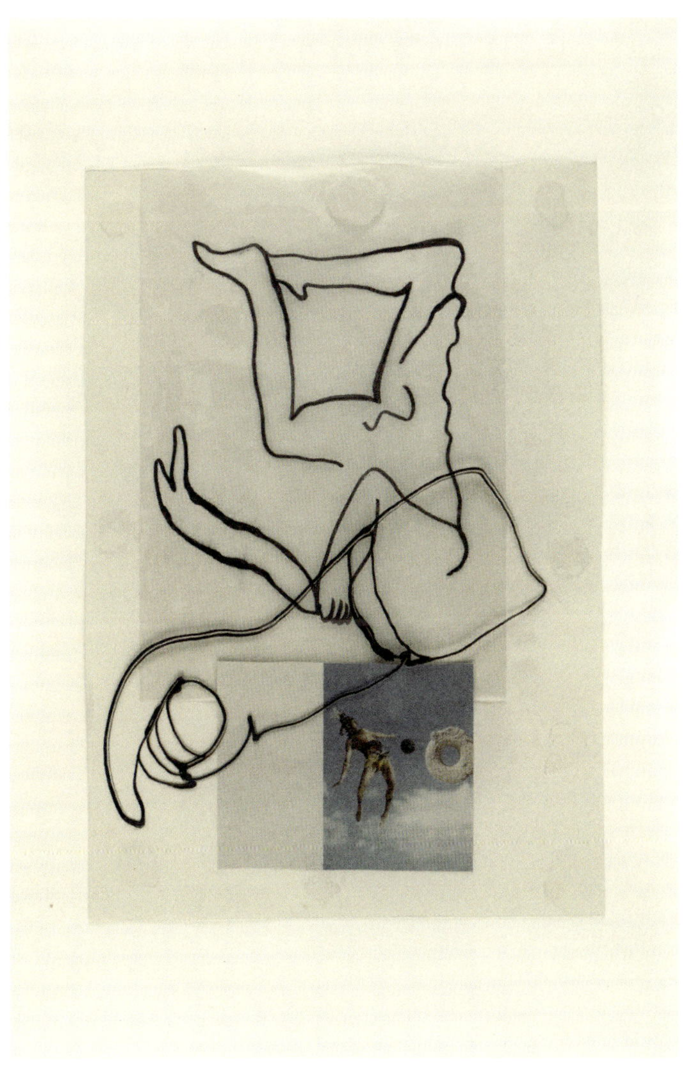

cat. 46

Mirte Van Duppen

print on seed sachet
63 mm × 80 mm
2016

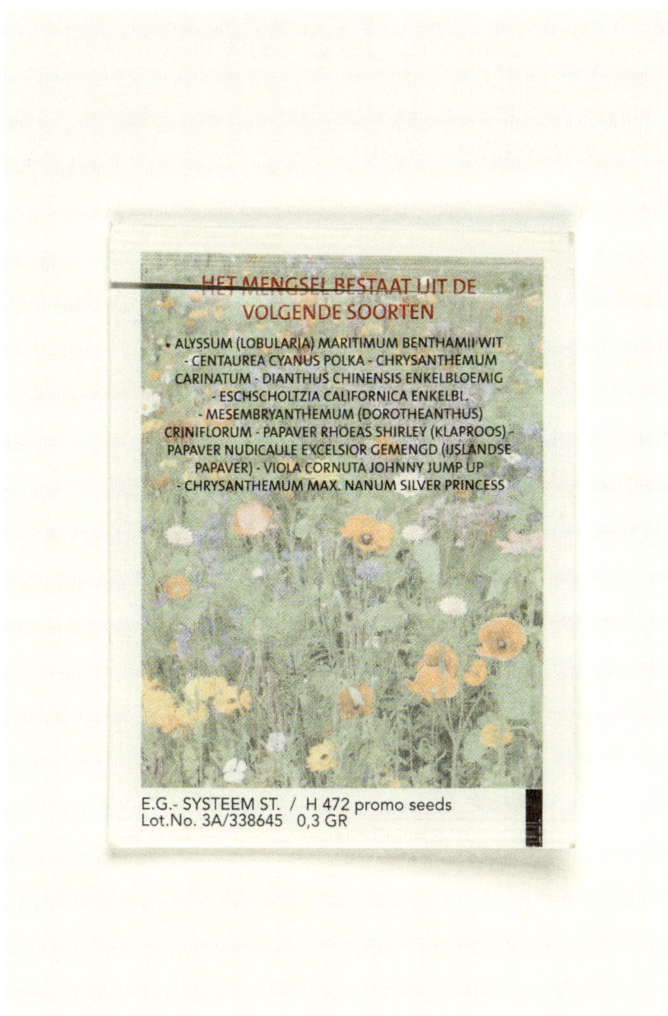
HET MENGSEL BESTAAT UIT DE
VOLGENDE SOORTEN
• ALYSSUM (LOBULARIA) MARITIMUM BENTHAMII WIT
- CENTAUREA CYANUS POLKA - CHRYSANTHEMUM
CARINATUM - DIANTHUS CHINENSIS ENKELBLOEMIG
- ESCHSCHOLTZIA CALIFORNICA ENKELBL.
- MESEMBRYANTHEMUM (DOROTHEANTHUS)
CRINIFLORUM - PAPAVER RHOEAS SHIRLEY (KLAPROOS) -
PAPAVER NUDICAULE EXCELSIOR GEMENGD (IJSLANDSE
PAPAVER) - VIOLA CORNUTA JOHNNY JUMP UP
- CHRYSANTHEMUM MAX. NANUM SILVER PRINCESS
E.G.- SYSTEEM ST. / H 472 promo seeds
Lot.No. 3A/338645 0,3 GR

cat. 47

Alice De Mont

photograph
200 mm × 109 mm
2016

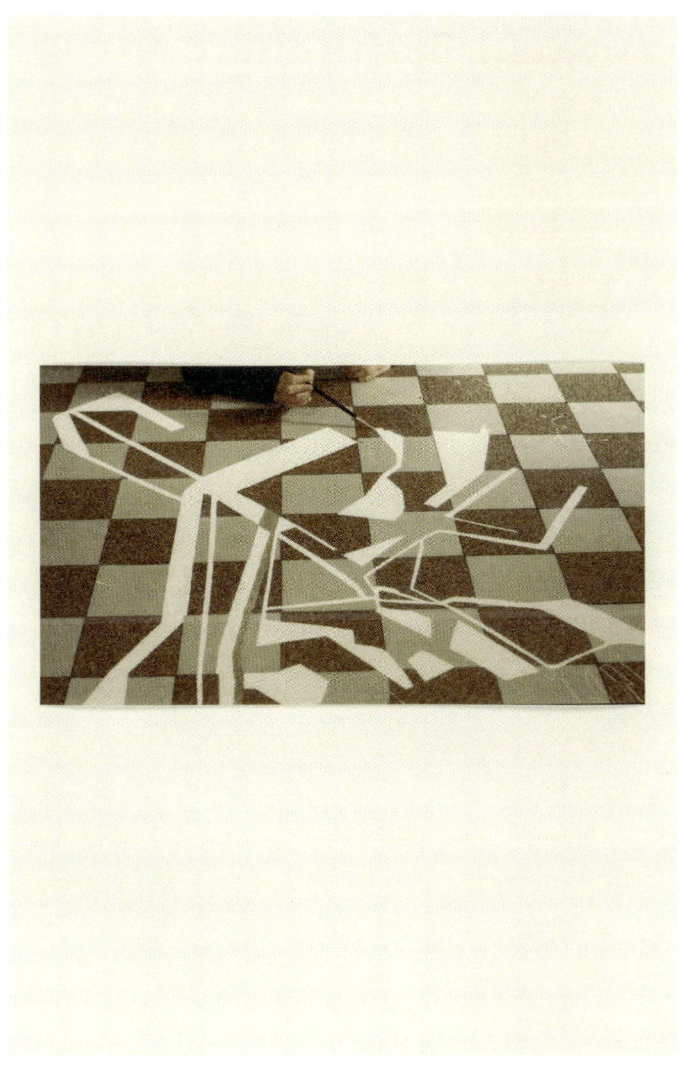

cat. 48

Alexis Lagimodière-Grisé

black backing
450 mm × 700 mm
2016

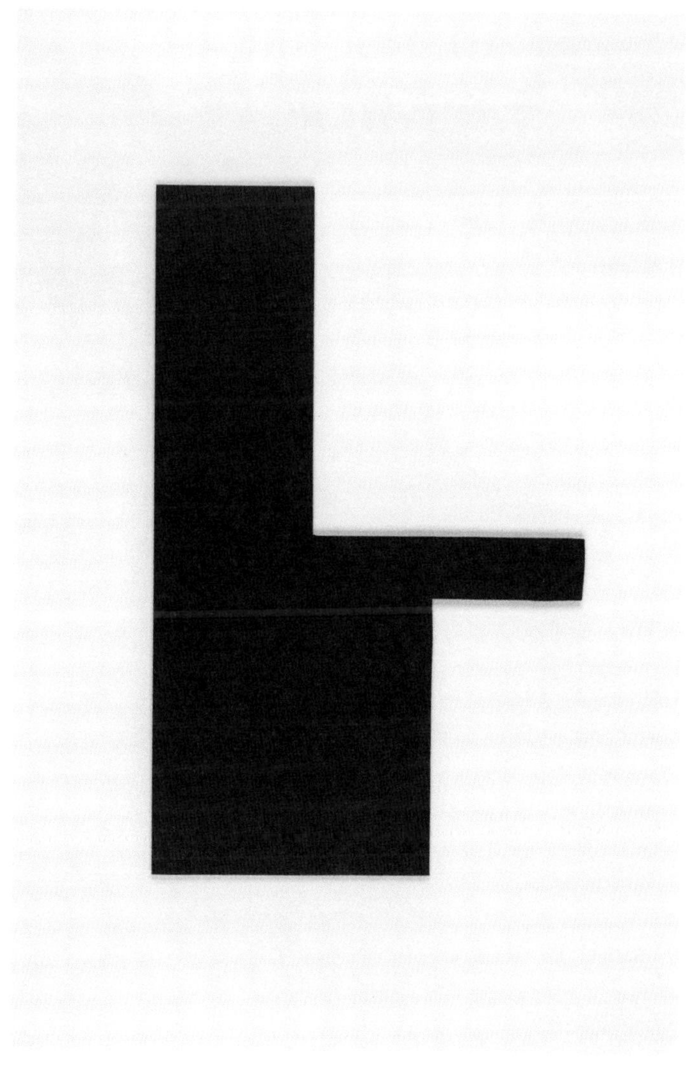

cat. 49

Ania Soliman
Frames

wooden frames, bubble wrap, tape
180 mm × 100 mm
2015

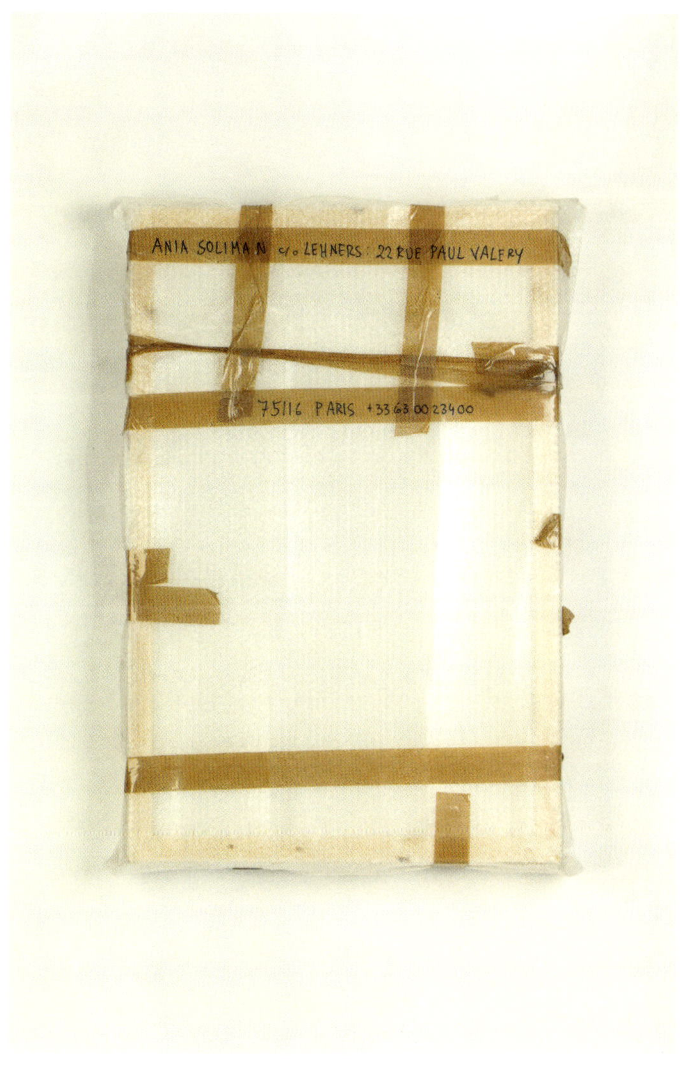

cat. 50

ANIA SOLIMAN c/o LEHNERS: 22 RUE PAUL VALERY
75116 PARIS +33 63 00 23400

Bisan Abu-Eisheh

photograph
$210\,\text{mm} \times 192\,\text{mm}$
2014

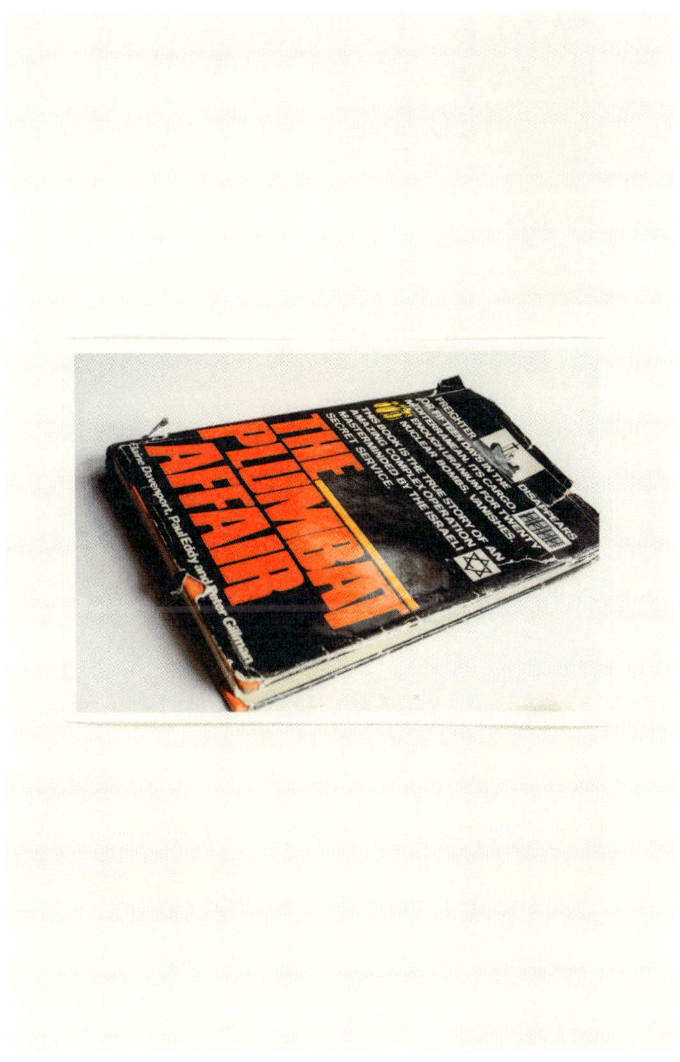
THE PLUMBAT AFFAIR
FREIGHTER DISAPPEARS
FOR FIFTEEN DAYS IN THE MEDITERRANEAN. ITS CARGO, ENOUGH URANIUM FOR TWENTY NUCLEAR BOMBS, VANISHES.
THIS BOOK IS THE TRUE STORY OF AN AMAZING COMPLEX OPERATION MASTERMINDED BY THE ISRAELI SECRET SERVICE.
Elaine Davenport, Paul Eddy and Peter Gillman

cat. 51

Augustas Serapinas

raincoat
dimensions variable
2016

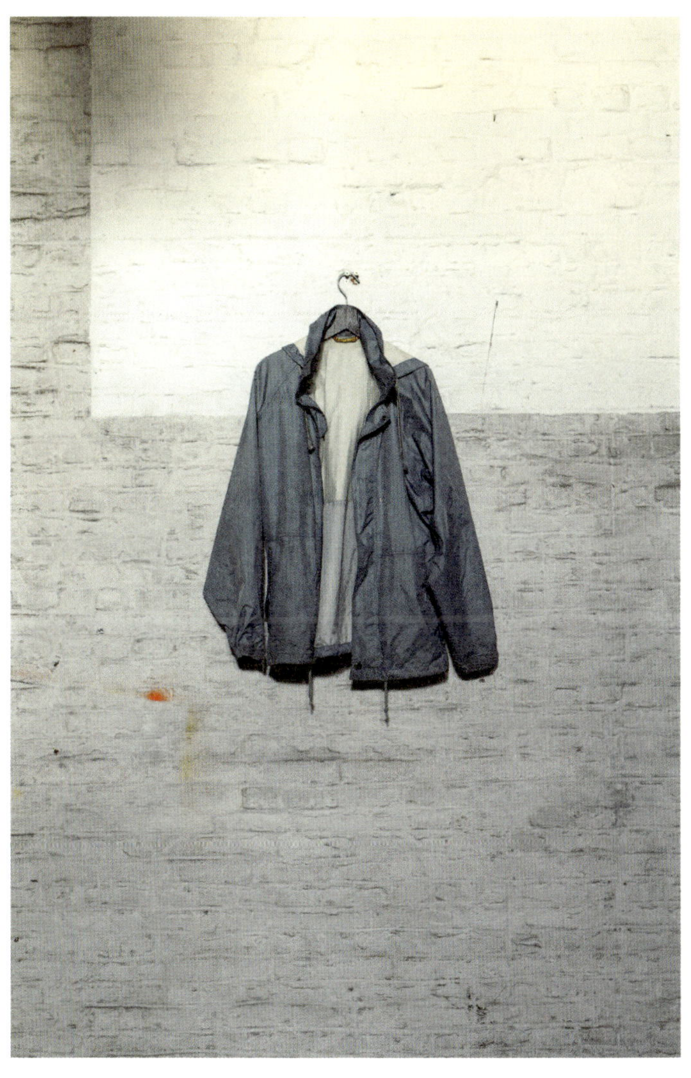

cat. 52

Stefanie Pretnar

coffee cup, token, match, shard
dimensions variable
2016

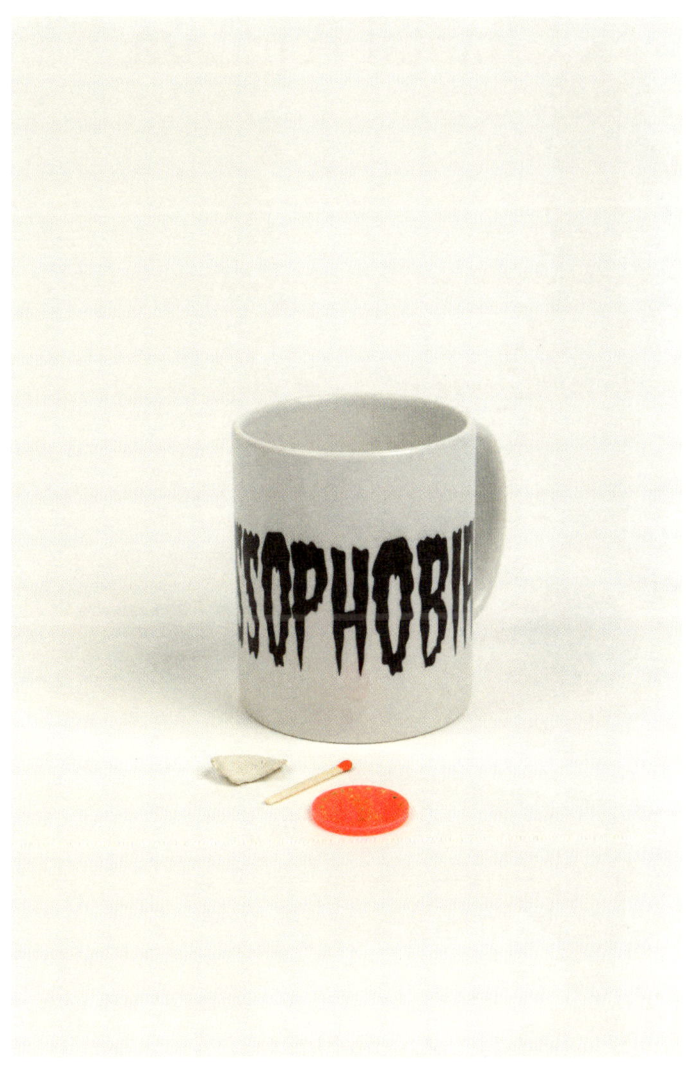

cat. 53

Chantal Peñalosa

chalk, chestnut
2016

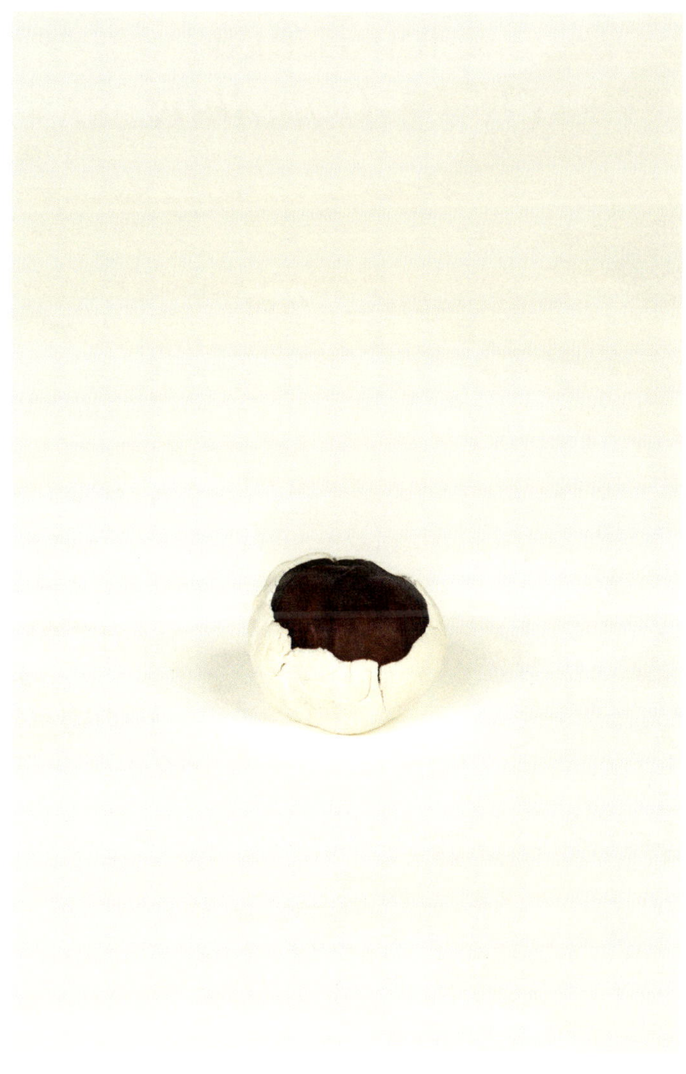

cat. 54

Elen Braga
Os 12 Trabalhos

metal, wire, screws, leather
dimensions variable
2017

cat. 55

Pages
Algorithmic Inhalation: 285 times Snapshot of the progression of opium smoke deposition in the human airways

print on paper
297 mm × 210 mm
2016

cat. 56

Leda Bourgogne
Staring back

acrylic on canvas
297 mm × 210 mm
2017

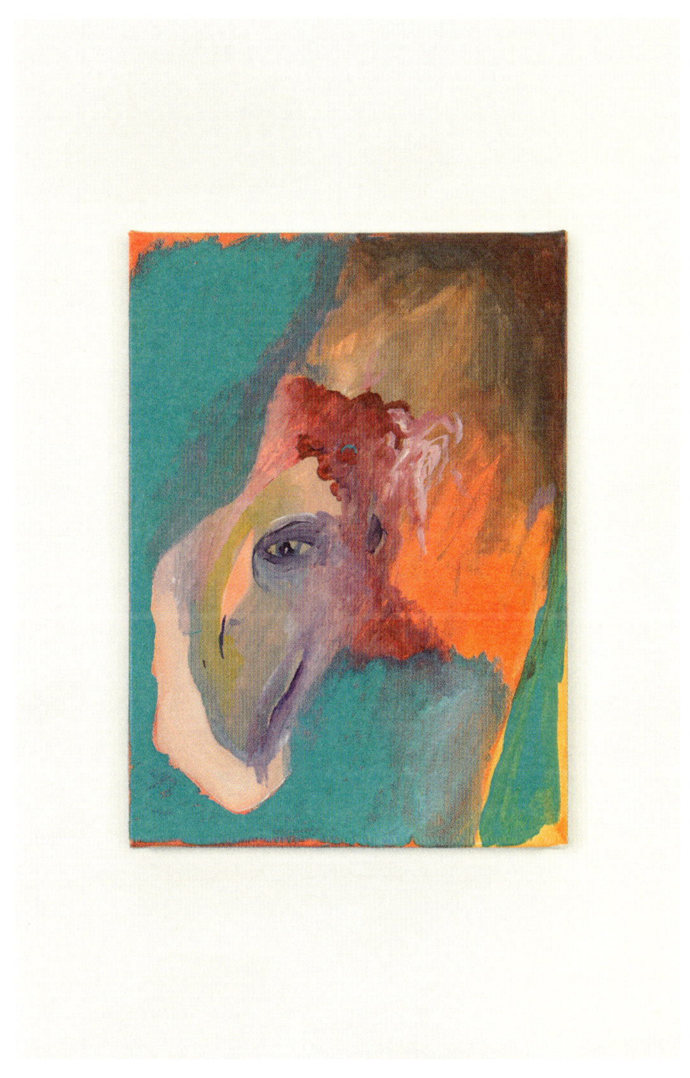

cat. 57

Paky Vlassopoulou

Cycling in high heels

red brick, duck tape

180 mm × 85 mm × 65 mm

2017

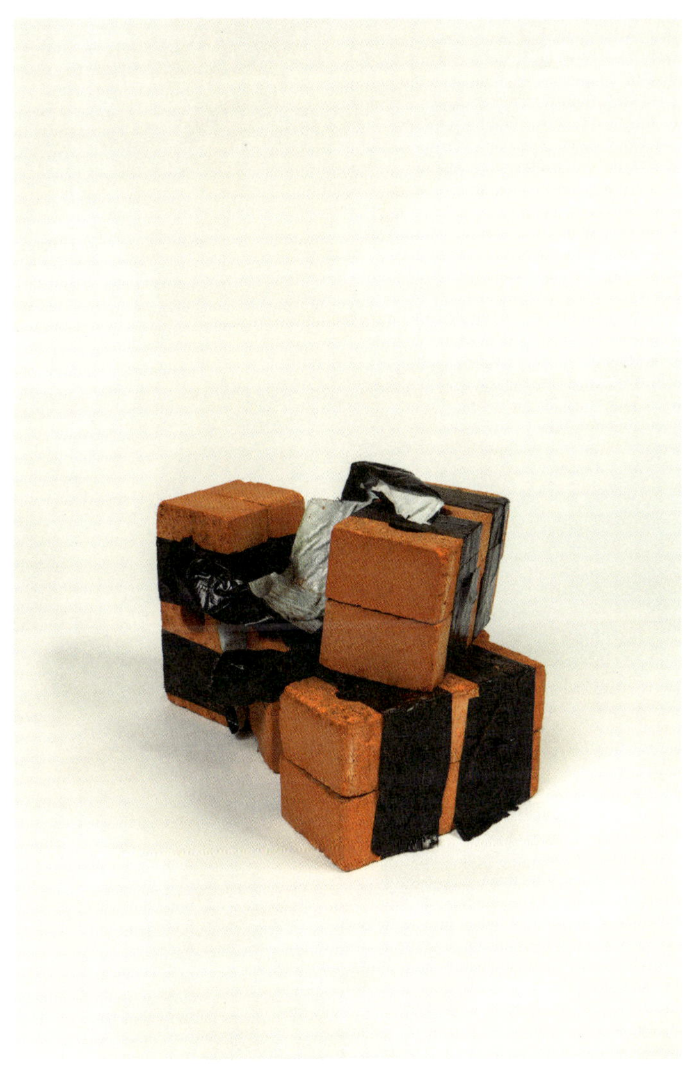

cat. 58

Romana Drdová
Vector for Egos

glue, wood
1000 mm × 150 mm
2018

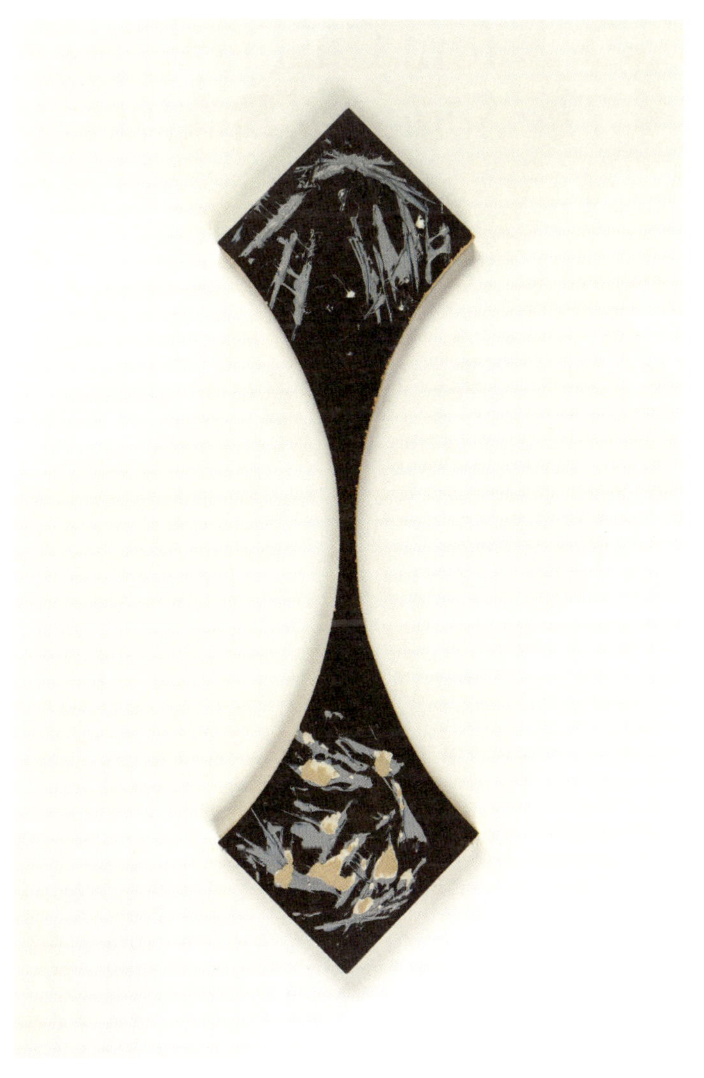

cat. 59

Tom Castinel
The Sound of Belgium

paint palette
297 mm × 210 mm
2017

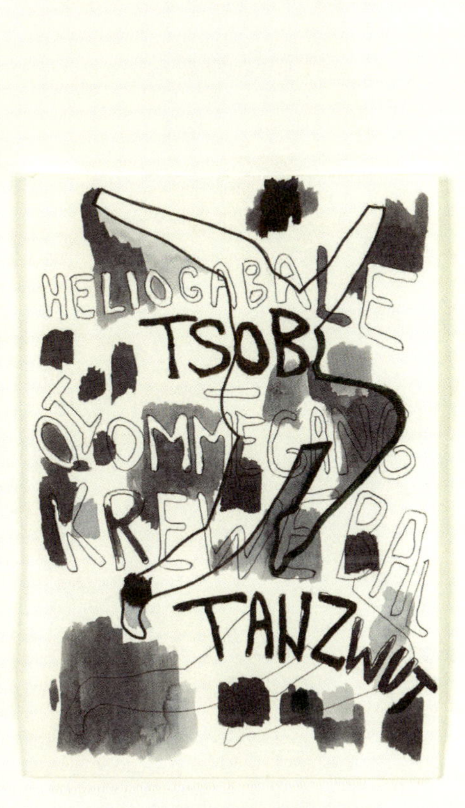

cat. 60

Sidney Aelbrecht
Venster

oil on canvas
60 mm × 60 mm
2018

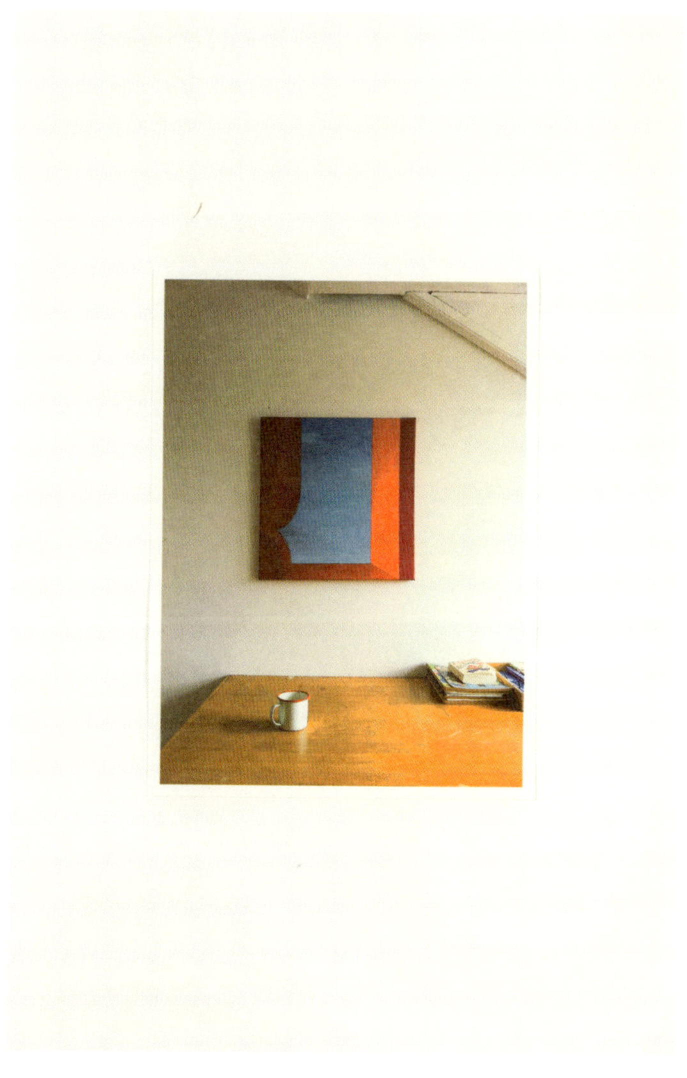

cat. 61

Eva L'Hoest

digital print, plexiglass
350 mm × 350 mm
2017

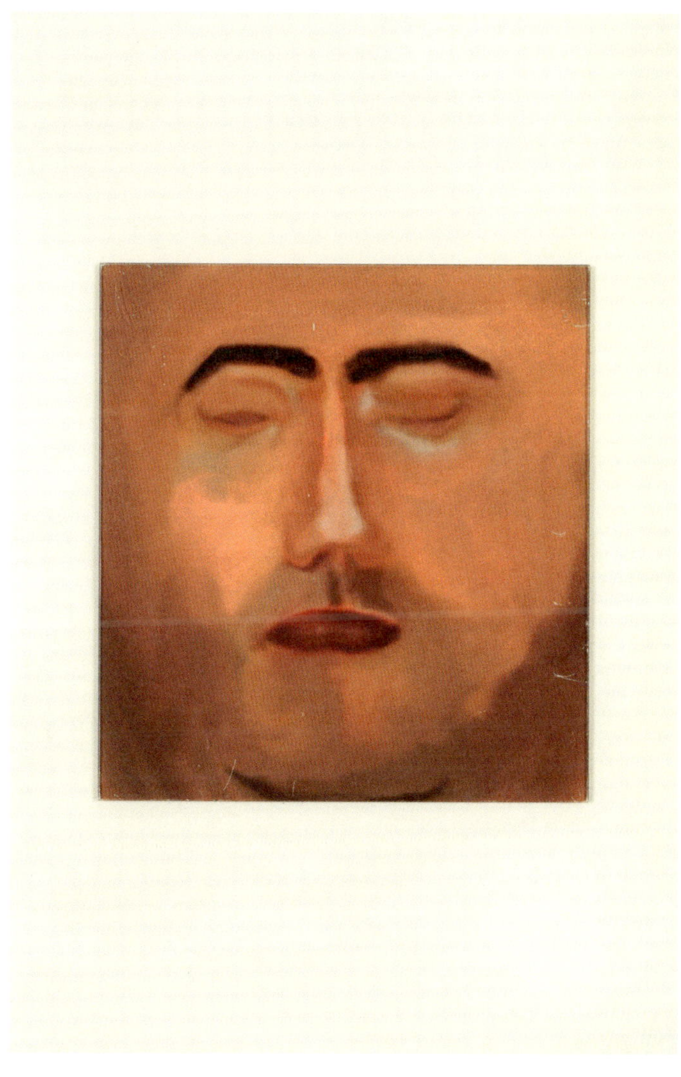

cat. 62

Line Boogaerts
Delight

cyanotype
297 mm × 210 mm
2018

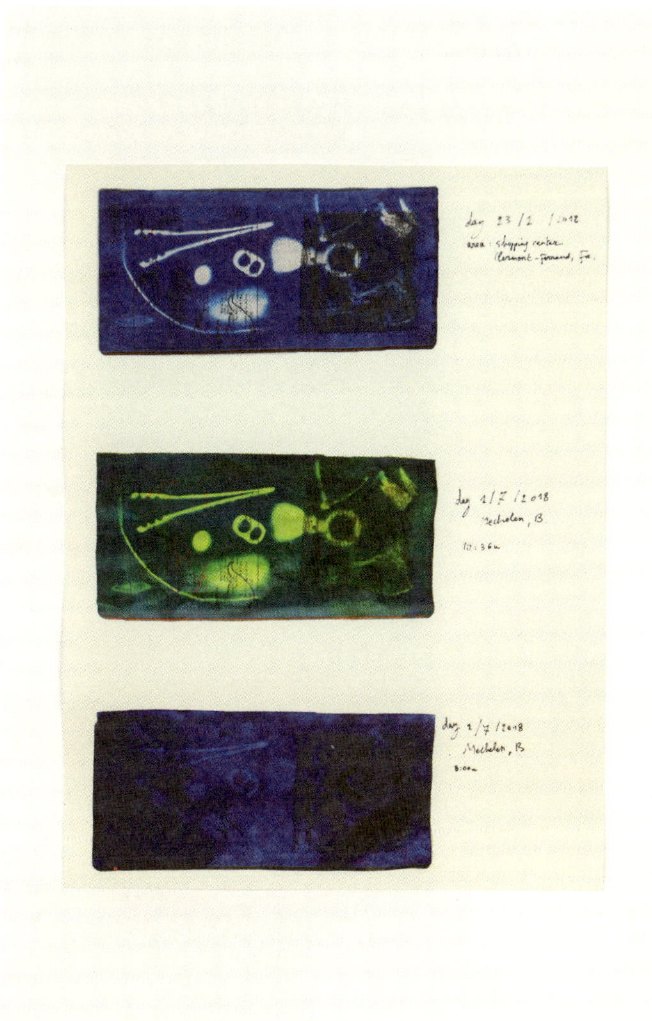

cat. 63

Ksenija Jovišević
Tourist Romantic

felt pen and pencil on paper
210 mm × 130 mm
2018

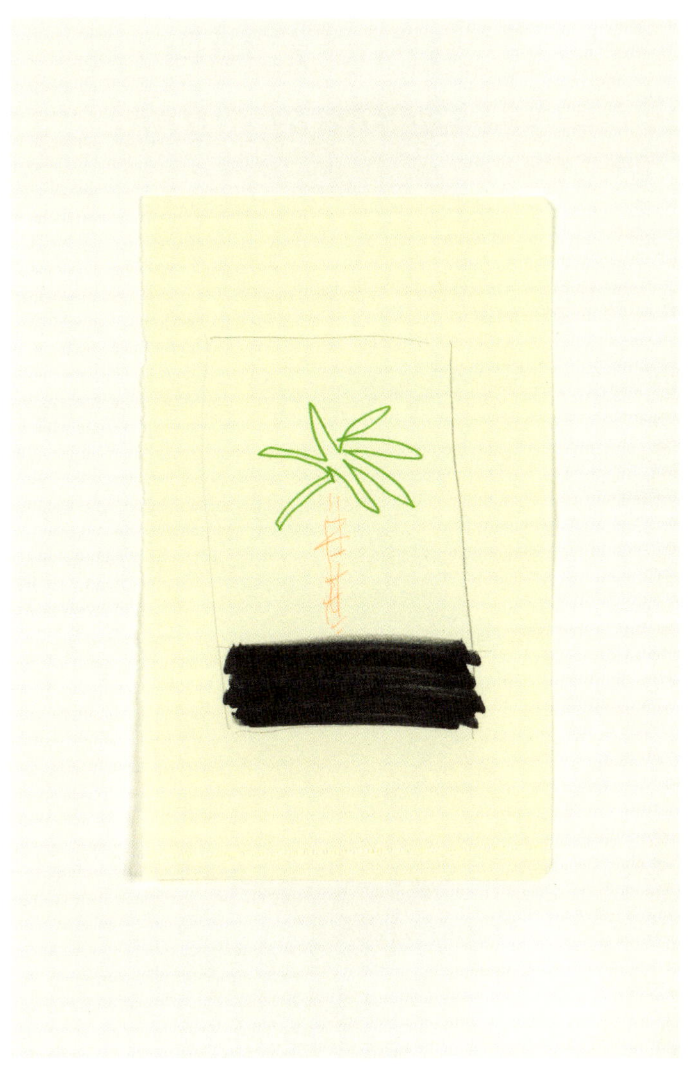

cat. 64

Bruno Zhu
roommate

dead insect
20 mm × 10 mm
2018

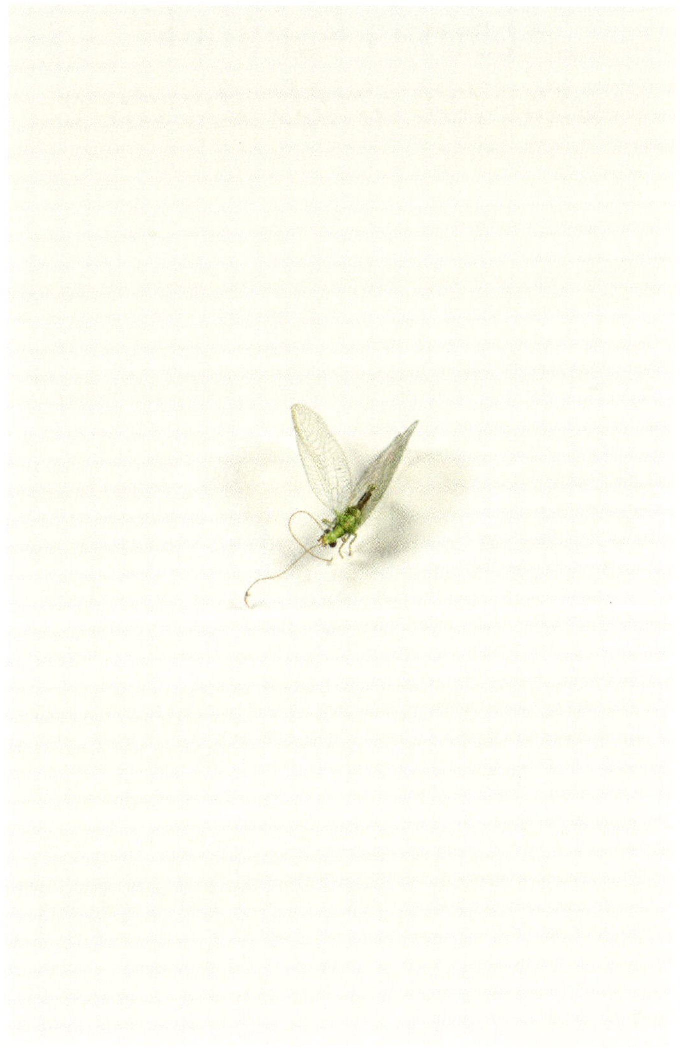

cat. 65

Tomáš Kajánek
Ancestor of 3D Printing

digital negative scan
220 mm × 190 mm
2017

cat. 66

Arnaud Eubelen
Friendly Carafe

plastic, concrete
150 mm × 150 mm
2017

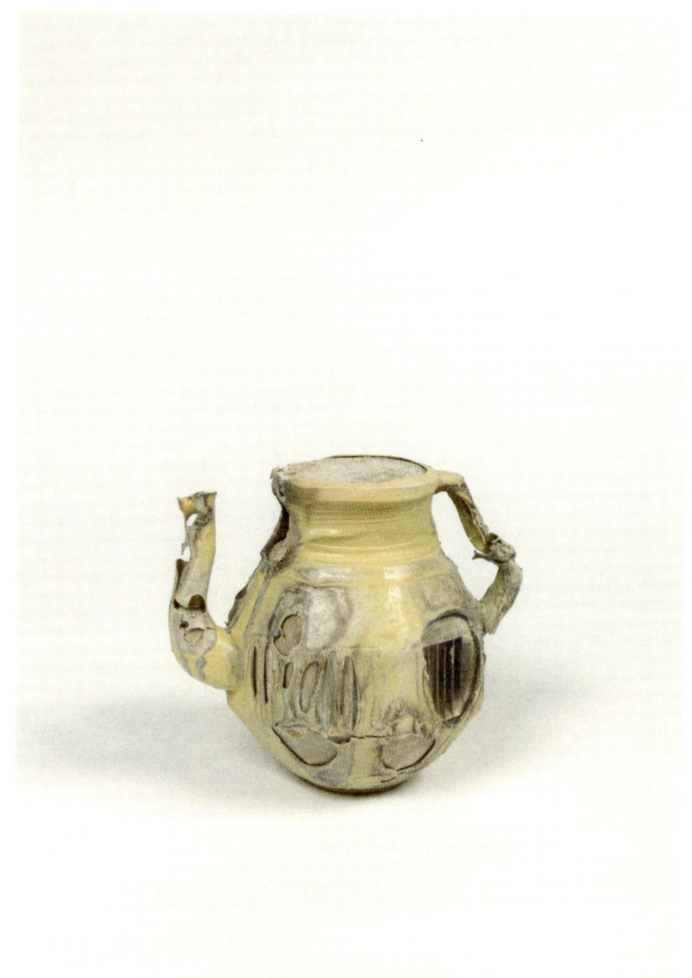

cat. 67

Stijn Van Dorpe

paper, pencil
297 mm × 210 mm
2017

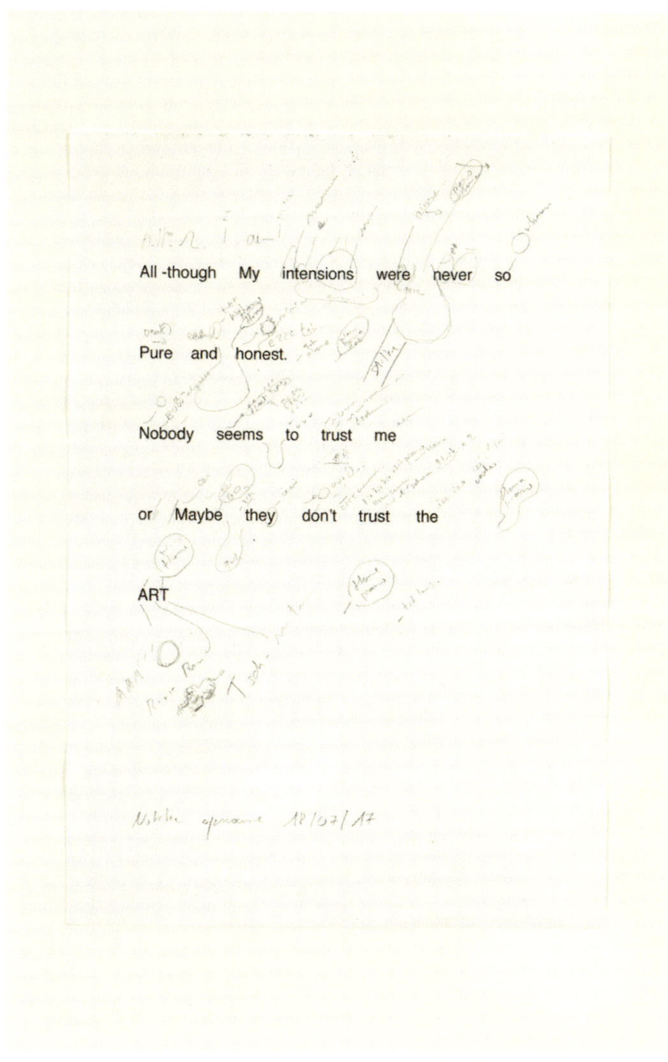
All -though My intensions were never so
Pure and honest.
Nobody seems to trust me
or Maybe they don't trust the
ART

cat. 68

Hemant Sareen
History, Place, Chance, Melancholia

pencil, postcard, publication 'W.G. Sebald, Austerlitz'
228,6 mm × 177,8 mm
2018

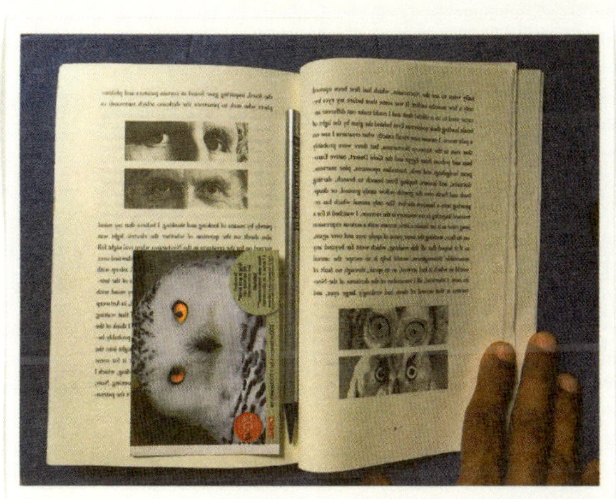

cat. 69

Maurice Doherty
Sacrifice

documentation of action: mosquito, artist's blood
10 mm × 5 mm
2018

cat. 70

Luisa Ungar
File: Lio resident at Antwerp zoo.jpg

a living monument to its own disappearance
210 mm × 297 mm
2017

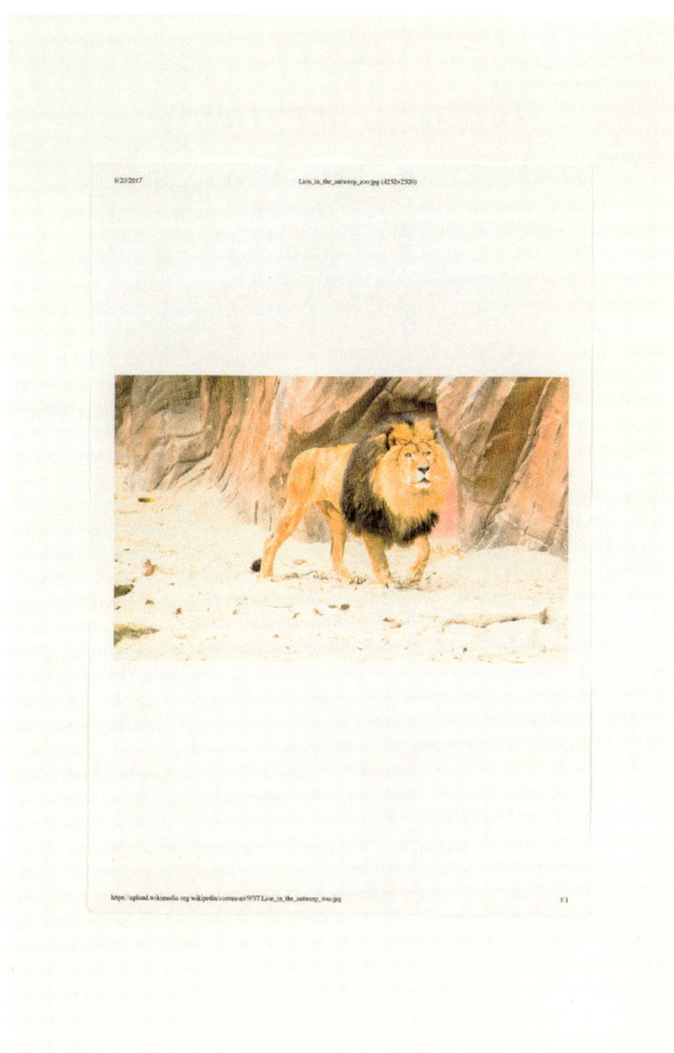

cat. 71

6/20/2017
Lion_in_the_antwerp_zoo.jpg (4252×2520)
https://upload.wikimedia.org/wikipedia/commons/9/97/Lion_in_the_antwerp_zoo.jpg
1/1

Geger
Digital Memory

smartphone photo
205 mm × 381 mm
2017

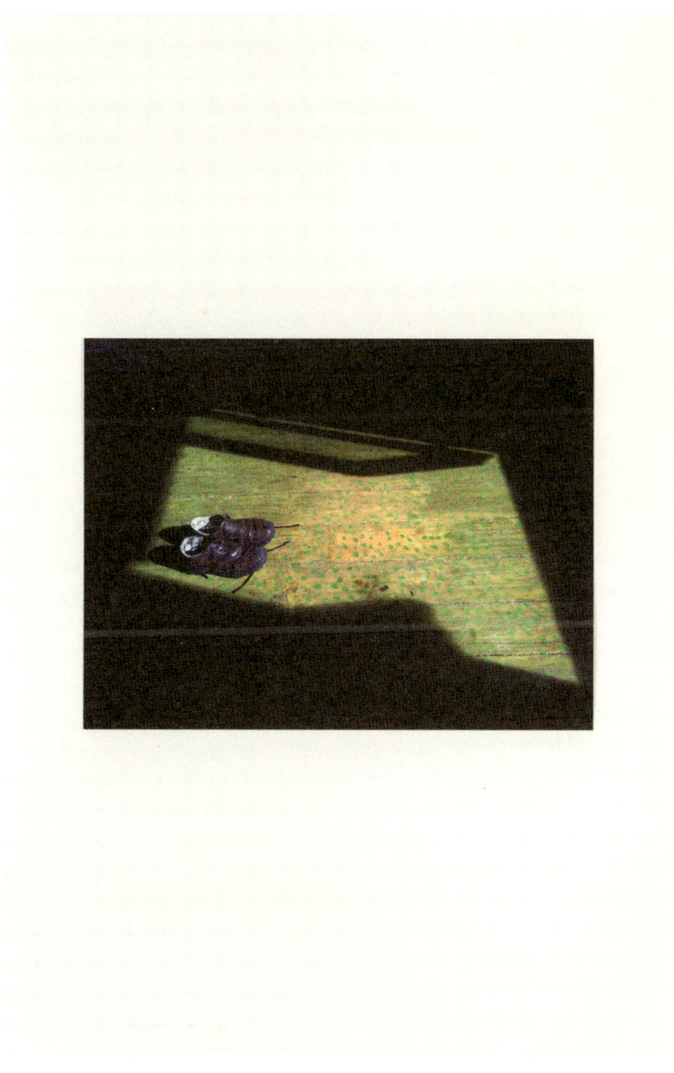

cat. 72

Nicolas Valckenaere
Newspaper after shirt

newspaper, acrylic, spraypaint
297 mm × 210 mm
2017

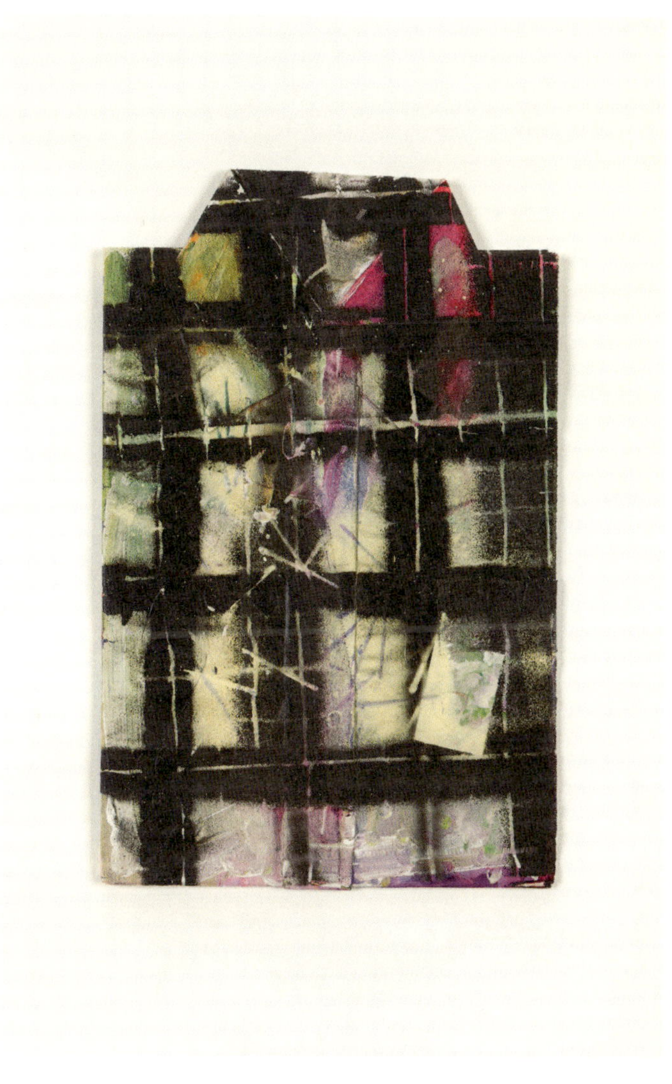

cat. 73

PEDIGREES OF OBJECTS
Interview with Clémentine Deliss, June 2016

AQ:

The idea for this conversation is the connection with the anthropologic but also, more specifically, because in your activities in the Weltkulturen Museum you worked with residencies. There you invited artists to actively work with the huge ethnographic collection of the Weltkulturen Museum and offer them the possibility to select some of these objects for 'a laboratory' on the ground floor of the residency (they lived on the second and first floors) so they could relate to these objects in an everyday manner. In your text, published recently in CAVE magazine, you mentioned an earlier residency program you organized in Edinburgh named Randolph Cliff.

CD:

From about 1996 onwards when I stopped making exhibitions as a curator, I wanted to define my work in terms of an extended relationship, a specific curatorial situation between artists in one location and artists in another. I became more interested in being an artist-to-artist curator working behind the scenes. It is 1996, so we don't have the kind of information circulating through the net about artists in different parts of the world. I just finished *Africa'95,* a big festival that included research in over 20 countries in Africa, and curated *Seven Stories about Modern Art in Africa* at the Whitechapel Art Gallery in London. I questioned the efficacy of an exhibition in the context of a curatorial project. I wanted to bring on the same level the models and conceptual ideas of artists working in different cities—moving between London and Dakar. That's when the relationship between workshops and residencies really started to become important and from 96 onwards I became a curator of people. I would curate gatherings. The very first one that made a significant change was *Tempolabor: a libertine laboratory*. Peter Pakesch, director of the Kunsthalle Basel at the time, asked me to do an exhibition and it was clear from the invitation that he wanted me to deal with the global situation. I thought it was irrelevant for me to do another exhibition in a Kunsthalle, with the same conditions and potential compromises, so I managed to get him to shift his budget from an exhibition format to a meeting behind closed doors. So in 1998 we held a gathering of one week in the old Warteck brewery building and in the Kunsthalle. It was a libertine laboratory, influenced by various writers like Crebillon Fils and others. In a private context we came together to speak about the things that aren't yet fully resolved, and to deal with the experiment of conversation. Artists and curators took part and were invited to present their work as if they were giving a lecture to the broad public. At that time there was no such thing as a 'performance lecture'. And if you look at the literature of the time, you will see that in 1998 you didn't have this heavily discursive context yet. It was quite a big move to denote a space within a museum or a Kunsthalle as if it were a discursive site that would normally be in a university context. I once wrote a text named *Curating with light luggage* where I speak about transvesting within institutions. In order to make a critique of an institution, you actually perform a different function within it. This has always interested me, seeing what happens if I put a university in a Kunsthalle, or a Kunsthalle in a university, which is what I was doing with Randolph Cliff. There I was working with the departments of engineering, robotics and neuroscience of the University of Edinburgh. For me, it has always been about finding a location that is in the dark, that no one is really looking at and finding ways to develop it so that it can re-emerge through the production process of artists. Randolph Cliff was a combination of needing to bring artists to Edinburgh and getting them to do downtime. It was part of the Future Academy project that I had been working on for seven years with the support of the University of Edinburgh and the College of Art.

Frankfurt

Then in 2010 I took on the job of director at the Weltkulturen Museum in Frankfurt. The public part of the museum was located in 3 separate buildings that were originally 19th century villas. Before I arrived, the staff had done everything they could to produce fake walls, lowering ceilings and thereby butchering the architecture not only of the museum but also of the villas. They made it incredibly ugly and tried to disguise the fact that they had to deal with a living space instead of an exhibition space. I returned it to its original function: to a domestic situation and then introduced the laboratory. I had written my PHD on French anthropology in the 1930s,when the idea of the laboratory was being developed around collections: e.g. The Mission Dakar-Djibouti. The amassing of objects from Africa was not only intended to create a new discipline of anthropology in the museum, but it was also a catalyst for new research. In Frankfurt, I wanted to re-introduce the workings of a laboratory because I wanted us to remediate the collection in a new way, through a new paradigm. The laboratory and the villa were part of what I call domestic research. It was essential for me that there would be artists in residence. The assignment was to come to the museum for a minimum of four weeks, to receive a fee, to work with the collection, to chose what one wanted to work with from the collection, to practically live with the collection. Each guest had an apartment, a studio and then the selection of objects down below in the lab. Out of this one might possibly produce some kind of prototypical thought or prototype product which then helped us to conceive an exhibition. It was not like a typical residency. For me a typical residency is a little bit along the lines of: 'Here is a space, you live in your studio, you have a sink in the corner, you meet people, you do an exhibition at the end, maybe there is a publication and you go back home again'. I wanted something much more precise, an engagement with the collection and I felt that the physical proximity between the resident and their selection was essential. There were moments when this didn't work and they were interesting too, but they had to be nipped in the bud. There was one artist who came over and said: 'it's fine, I'll take pictures, we will do a 3D scan of objects etcetera and then I will go back to New York and send you the work'. And that was NO… Or another one who said 'yes I can only come for a couple of days, but I know what I am going to do, we are going to take all the baskets that you have and put them in the exhibition space'. NO! I needed the recursive approach. I needed rectification, additions, discussions, and engagement with those material things, with their stubbornness, their material presence.

The pedigrees of objects

AQ:

Another element that I found very interesting is 'the production of alternative narratives', because by offering this sort of framework it allows the artist to do something extraordinary. Their research also led you to a better insight of the collection.

CD:

Sure, it is an extraordinary phenomenon that these huge collections, which exist in Belgium as well, are practically unresearched. In other words, the discipline of museum anthropology is the dominant key into their interpretation. You use this key to enter a house. Not much has been written on these objects at all because it is channelled through ethnographic methodologies or approaches in anthropology, which are generally speaking connected to the description of ethnic groups or 'source communities' and how they live and operate. An object becomes an illustration of a wider understanding of a culture, a group of people, or a phenomenon. These objects are in an orphan-like state, with an absence of sufficient information. If you bring in someone who creates a heterodox assemblage and places different artefacts into an unexpected correlation or set of correspondences then, in this elliptical way, it's possible to create new interpretations. This process can happen on many different levels. It can happen like it did with artist Peggy Buth who managed to create assemblages of missionary photography that allowed us to look at them anew. This also happened with the exhibition *Object Atlas,* and the work of Antje Majewski or Simon Popper in particular, who started painting the objects. One of the problems is that we have trouble looking at the physicality of objects today. This is where photography comes into play.

Photographic representation

The photography question in 'tribal art' is based on a particular type of photography: the classic approach, which aims to develop an auratic frame around an object. A dark background, spotlights and a particular type of focus that pumps up the visual volume, provides a new patina, or glamour to an object that looks potentially frumpy and uninteresting when it has been removed from its original site. The use of photography enables us to look at the subject in a different way. That was a very important entry, which the work at the Weltkulturen Museum revealed. Peggy Buth was one of the most brilliant artists in the Weltkulturen lab, because she found ways to help us understand what we were looking at. That's one way of dealing with it: the communicative or dialogical aspect of working with artists.

Access to the object

The other aspect is something I could never really fully develop, but which remains an interesting one: given the fact that we don't know much about these objects, but that they are there, and given the fact that we cannot repatriate them in one go, and we wouldn't know who to repatriate them too exactly and where that would be... if we enabled access to them, which is exactly what isn't happening at the moment, then it might be possible for people, whether they are from the source community or not, to at least work on them and create derivative objects from them. In other words: you can patent a new object that is derived from a single or historical piece, if you have a proof of technicity. Therefore if somebody develops a structure for a housing model or a fiber structure that can be used in deep sea diving or anything on the basis of their access and research on collections, and this research has proof of technicity, the reappropriation of that object can happen through a new generation that has been created from it, out of it, out of the original. This I find really intriguing. The laboratory that we worked on in the museum was not only about artists experimenting and creating new narrotological vehicles. It was about all the ramifications of what they were doing that would enter into a museum context, such as: What is the value of the object they leave behind? What is the nature of the legal status of this object in relation to the original that has been worked from? What is the state of provenance of the artists who have worked with these objects? What about patenting and copyright? All of these issues can enter the debate and eventually begin to change the nature of how we conceive a museum experience. Working with a domestic scale, the house, with the objects, the third space of the lab that is neither the exhibition nor storage, but an area where the guest can create an assemblage didn't only lead to an exhibition and the extension of the collection. It led to a whole bunch of questions that were the ramification of a new kind of understanding of an institution. This began with the architectonic, with saying: in this museum we need places where people can work without being exhibited. We need a place to place the objects before they are shown. We need to consider the financial value created by an artist who produces a prototype in relation to an object they have studied. We need to think about how to evaluate this. What is the value of the object that is left behind in a collection for which the evaluation of the ethnographic object is already problematic? So what is the value of the work left by Otobong Nkanga? Do I base this on a hierarchy of private galleries, of the artists that I work with? No, I can't. What is the logic, with which we will define the value of this object? It's not twice the fee that the museum provided, it's not what her gallery would charge. What is it? What is the capital that is being produced here? So all these questions for me had more to do with the negotiation of a new kind of institutional organism.

Value of objects

AQ:

That's very interesting, because the artists who

work with these objects also provide a new pedigree, so the value also changes. The status of that object changes. It is not only part of a huge collection, but it establishes another chapter.

CD:

Value in ethnographic museums is based on provenance. If you have an object, let's take this one [takes a stapler]. All you know is that it was collected in 1874 during an expedition and you think it was from this part of Angola or this part of Zimbabwe and you think it might be something used in warfare, right? If this object has more provenance, in other words, it was once sold to another museum, or it was once sold to someone like Nelson Rockefeller or Estee Lauder or passed through the hands of famous people, then it will be valued more highly then when there is absolutely no trace.

The exclusion of traces

The difficulty that you have with the discourse of museum anthropology is that it excludes certain traces to the benefit of other areas of knowledge. The resistance I encountered at the Weltkulturen Museum from the custodians had a lot to do with the legitimation of artists I invited and the acccss to the objects that I gave them. This was the key determinant of meaning and it offered alternative methodologies of interpretation. There was a disregard of how to classify these objects following the existing canon of anthropology. When the artists produced new works, and donated these to the museum, the custodians had trouble accepting them. What region does it belong too, they asked.

It has nothing to do with Latin America, because the artist is German, because the artist is Nigerian, so who deals with it? So eventually, a small little filing cabinet was produced for the lab works. It was depressing. Serious classification was practically impossible. I discovered unfinished inventorization. The old guard of custodians wouldn't deal with it, they would hand it over to an intern, as if it was really secondary.

So they did not recognize that, if Otobong Nkanga, Thomas Bayrle, Marc Camille Chaimovicz or Peggy Buth, activated the object again, that was also part of provenance? They were very unaccepting of the generating production of meaning that people other than anthropologists were able to provide.

The new collection

AQ:

This leads to the future of the anthropological collection. You mentioned this also in your writings: the growth of these collections are questioned, partly because of how they originated, but also in a lot of cases you cannot bring the object back to its origins. How do you consider the future of the anthropological collection? How do you think it could still grow? Would you consider the traces brought together in this publication as a possible growth of the collection?

CD:

Hmmm, you need to enable access. If one begins to invite architects not to build museums, but to build intelligent depots, then this is possible. No one hears about an architect building a depot! Generally speaking the focus is all on the presentation of these objects. Lots of debates about how to present them best, how to create an interactive environment, how to address people today in 2017, within a different geopolitical situation. The thinking behind the exhibition of these collections is dominant. One needs a new building, one needs to show people collections, one needs to present the work, but how do we do this? What are the themes? In Frankfurt, we moved away from just showing Swahili culture or Yoruba culture. Today objects play in many ways a secondary role. They become illustrations. If you were to put the emphasis on the 99,9% of objects that are not displayed and if you provide access to them in order to develop new interpretations around them you will already be making a new collection. You don't need to buy more objects for this collection. You need to provide access and an openness towards their potential for new interpretations. Then there is a proliferation of meanings across time.

Who do you allow in?

You have to imagine the severity of the frame within which these objects are still considered. Imagine if we started to circulate these objects, imagine if history museums like the national museum of Kiev sent a collection to the ethnographic museum of Tervuren. You could send some of the objects gathered in the Belgian Congo to Kiev, and then from Kiev to Bangladesh. These kinds of shifts are no different from the shifts of people who are moving around today. But sadly there isn't actually any kind of attempt to think through the migration of collections. We need to recognize, once and for all, that these are the worlds' histories of aesthetics, of methods and solutions to the experiments of life practices that include every single dimension of what we do, how we live etc. We have to recognize the value of these objects, films and photographs in acquiring a freedom of interpretation and a freedom of access. We, with our museums, have no right to embargo these objects any longer.

INDEX OF ARTISTS 2013 – 2018

NAME	ORIGIN	CURRENT	PERIOD OF RESIDENCY	RESIDENCY PLACE
Mounira Al Solh	Lebanon	Amsterdam	07.12 – 12.12	Antwerp
Liesje De Laet	Belgium	Antwerp	09.12 – 11.12	Fondation Mercier, Sierre
Francesc Ruiz	Spain	Barcelona	09.12 – 10.12	Antwerp
Isabelle Schiltz	Belgium	Brussels	10.12 – 01.13	Antwerp
Philip Janssens	Belgium	Brussels	11.12 – 03.13	Antwerp
Pedro Barateiro	Portugal	Lisbon	11.12 – 05.13	Antwerp
Edgardo Aragón	Mexico	Oaxaca	01.13 – 03.13	Antwerp
Lou Hubbard	Australia	Melbourne	03.13 – 06.13	Antwerp
Darren Roshier	Switzerland	Sierre	01.13 – 03.13	Antwerp
Ilaria Lupo	Italy	Beirut	01.13 – 04.13	Antwerp
Naneci Yurdagül	Turkey	Frankfurt am Main	04.13 – 06.13	Antwerp
Luciana Lamothe	Argentina	Mercedes	04.13 – 06.13	Antwerp
Post Brothers	USA	San Francisco	05.13 – 07.13	Antwerp
Stine Marie Jacobsen	Denmark	Berlin	07.13 – 12.13	Antwerp
Sarah Hendrickx	Belgium	Antwerp	09.13 – 11.13	Fondation Mercier, Sierre
Bhagwati Prasad	India	New Delhi	09.13 – 11.13	Antwerp
Mark Luyten	Belgium	Antwerp	10.13	Beirut
Rumiko Hagiwara	Japan	Amsterdam	10.13 – 12.13	Antwerp

NAME	ORIGIN	CURRENT	PERIOD OF RESIDENCY	RESIDENCY PLACE
Mathilde Du Sordet	France	Lyon	10.13 – 12.13	Antwerp / Artistes en Résidence, Clermont-Ferrand
Kato Six	Belgium	Brussels	12.13 – 03.14	Antwerp / Artistes en Résidence Clermont-Ferrand
Reg Carremans	Belgium	Brussels	01.14 – 06.14	Antwerp
Claire Liengme	Switzerland	Sierre	01.14 – 03.14	Antwerp
Kasper Bosmans	Belgium	Brussels	02.14 – 03.14	R.A.V.I., Liège
Xavier Mary	Belgium	Liège	02.14	Antwerp
Jonathan De Winter	Belgium	Liège	02.14	Antwerp
Fabian Rouwette	Belgium	Liège	03.14	Antwerp
Antoine Van Impe	Belgium	Liège	03.14	Antwerp
Philippe Van Wolputte	Belgium	Antwerp	03.14	R.A.V.I., Liège
Laure Prouvost	France	London	03.14 – 07.14	Antwerp
Augustas Serapinas	Lithuania	Vilnius	04.14 – 09.14	Antwerp
Carla Filipe	Portugal	Porto	04.14 – 09.14	Antwerp
Juha Pekka Matias Laakkonen	Finland	Sweden	04.14 – 05.14	Antwerp
Oscar Murillo	Columbia	New York	06.14	Antwerp
Savage	United Kingdom	Bristol	07.14 – 10.14	Antwerp
Nicholas Hoffman	USA	Vienna	07.14 – 10.14	Antwerp

NAME	ORIGIN	CURRENT	PERIOD OF RESIDENCY	RESIDENCY PLACE
Bert Jacobs	Belgium	Brussels	09.14 – 11.14	AIR_Frankfurt, Frankfurt am Main
Simon Feydieu	France	Lyon	10.14 – 01.15	Artistes en Résidence Clermont-Ferrand
Stefanie Pretnar	Germany	Frankfurt am Main	10.14 – 12.14	Antwerp
Jane Coppin	Belgium	Bekegem	01.15 – 12.15	Antwerp
Elise Eeraerts	Belgium	Antwerp	01.15 – 12.15	Antwerp
Karolien Chromiak	Belgium	Antwerp	01.15 – 12.15	Antwerp
Lore Van Roelen	Belgium	Antwerp	01.15 – 12.15	Antwerp
Daan Gielis	Belgium	Antwerp	01.15 – 12.15	Antwerp
Joris De Rycke	Belgium	Antwerp	11.14 – 02.15	Antwerp / Artistes en Résidence, Clermont-Ferrand
Bisan Abu-Eisheh	Palestine	Jerusalem / Glasgow	11.14	Antwerp
Nihan Somay	Turkey	Istanbul	01.15 – 03.15	Antwerp
Ania Soliman	Irak / USA	New York	01.15 – 04.15	Antwerp
David Armstrong Six	Canada	Montreal	02.15 – 05.15	Antwerp
Bianca Baldi	South-Africa	Frankfurt am Main	02.15 – 07.15	Antwerp
Timo Van Grinsven	The Netherlands	Antwerp	04.15 – 06.15	AIR_Frankfurt, Frankfurt am Main
Rasmus Søndergaard Johanssen	Denmark	Frankfurt am Main	04.15 – 06.15	Antwerp

NAME	ORIGIN	CURRENT	PERIOD OF RESIDENCY	RESIDENCY PLACE
Donna Kukama	South-Africa	Johannesburg	04.15 – 06.15	Antwerp
Shelbatra Jashari	Belgium	Brussels	05.15 – 07.15	Antwerp
Pieter Huybrechts	Belgium	Antwerp	05.15	Kooshk Residency, Tehran
Yan Tomaszewski	France / Poland	Paris	07.15 – 10.15	Antwerp
Volker Zander	Germany	Cologne	08.15 – 10.15	Antwerp
Maryam Ashkanian	Iran	Tehran	08.15	Antwerp
Jane Coppin	Belgium	Bekegem	09.15 – 11.15	Fondation Mercier, Sierre
Nel Aerts	Belgium	Antwerp	10.15 – 12.15	Van Goghhuis, Zundert
Lennart Lahuis	The Netherlands	Paris	10.15 – 12.15	Antwerp
Dirk Van Lieshout	The Netherlands	Rotterdam	10.15 – 01.16	Antwerp
Sol Archer	United Kingdom	Rotterdam	10.15 – 01.16	Antwerp
Bik Van der Pol	The Netherlands	Rotterdam	12.15	Antwerp
Baptiste Croze	France	Madrid / Marseille	10.15 – 01.16	Antwerp / Artistes en Résidence Clermont-Ferrand
Lodewijk Heylen	Belgium	Turnhout / Antwerp	11.15 – 02.16	Antwerp / Artistes en Résidence Clermont-Ferrand
Lieven Segers	Belgium	Antwerp	01.16 – 03.16	Van Goghhuis, Zundert

NAME	ORIGIN	CURRENT	PERIOD OF RESIDENCY	RESIDENCY PLACE
Niek Hendrix	The Netherlands	Maastricht	01.16 – 03.16	Antwerp
Robert Šalanda	Czech Republic	Prague	01.16 – 06.16	Antwerp / MeetFactory Prague
Alice De Mont	Belgium	Ghent	01.16 – 06.16	Antwerp / MeetFactory Prague
Timo Van Grinsven	The Netherlands	Antwerp	01.16 – 12.16	Antwerp
mountaincutters	France	Brussels / Marseille	01.16 – 12.16	Antwerp
Jim Campers	Belgium	Antwerp	01.16 – 12.16	Antwerp
Ode De Kort	Belgium	Antwerp	01.16 – 12.16	Antwerp
Maika Garnica	Belgium	Antwerp	01.16 – 12.16	Antwerp
Ghislain Amar	France	Rotterdam	01.16 – 03.16	AIR_Frankfurt, Frankfurt am Main
Levent Kunt	Germany	Frankfurt am Main	01.16 – 03.16	Pavilioen a/h Water, Rotterdam
Stijn Van Dorpe	Belgium	Ghent	01.16 – 03.16	Pavilioen a/h Water, Rotterdam
Gauthier Oushoorn	Belgium	Brussels	02.16	Kooshk Residency, Tehran
Albert Mayr	Austria	Vienna	04.16	Antwerp
Alberto García del Castillo	Spain	Brussels	04.16 – 05.16	Antwerp
Mirthe Van Duppen	The Netherlands	Rotterdam	04.16 – 06.16	Antwerp

NAME	ORIGIN	CURRENT	PERIOD OF RESIDENCY	RESIDENCY PLACE
Karl Philips	Belgium	Hasselt	04.16 – 06.16	AIR_Frankfurt, Frankfurt am Main
Ani Schulze	Germany	Frankfurt am Main	04.16 – 06.16	Antwerp
Luis Lázaro Matos	Portugal	Lisbon	04.16 - 05.16	Antwerp
Alexis Lagimodière-Grisé	Canada	New York	06.16 – 09.16	Antwerp
Serra Tansel	Turkey	London	06.16 – 07.16	Antwerp
Peter Fengler	The Netherlands	Rotterdam	07.16	Antwerp
Marie Zolamian	Lebanon	Liège	07.16 – 09.16	Antwerp
Jayne Dent	United Kingdom	Newcastle	07.16 – 09.16	Antwerp
Diango Hernandez	Cuba	Düsseldorf	08.16 – 10.16	Antwerp
Anna Pöhlmann	Germany	Düsseldorf	08.16 – 10.16	Antwerp
Roya Keshavarz	Iran	Tehran	08.16	Antwerp
Chantal Peñalosa	Mexico	Tijuana	09.16 – 11.16	Antwerp
Elen Braga	Brazil	Brussels	10.16 – 12.16	Antwerp
Babak Afrassiabi	Iran	Rotterdam	11.16 – 01.17	Antwerp
Nasrin Tabatabai	Iran	Rotterdam	11.16 – 01.17	Antwerp
Pierre Clèment	France	Lyon	11.16 – 02.17	Antwerp / Artistes en Résidence Clermont-Ferrand

NAME	ORIGIN	CURRENT	PERIOD OF RESIDENCY	RESIDENCY PLACE
Liesbet Grupping	Belgium	Antwerp	11.16 – 02.17	Antwerp / Artistes en Résidence Clermont-Ferrand
Nicolas Valckenaere	Belgium	Stoumont	12.16 – 02.17	Antwerp / Stoumont
Tomáš Kajánek	Czech Republic	Prague	01.17 – 06.17	Antwerp / MeetFactory, Prague
Stijn Van Dorpe	Belgium	Ghent	01.17 – 06.17	Antwerp / MeetFactory Prague
Kitty Kamp	Belgium	Brussels	01.17 – 12.17	Antwerp
Polien Boons	Belgium	Mechelen	01.17 – 12.17	Antwerp
Amber Vanluffelen	Belgium	Antwerp	01.17 – 12.17	Antwerp
Karen Moser	Switzerland	Antwerp	01.17 – 12.17	Antwerp
Mathieu Verhaeghe	Belgium	Antwerp	01.17 – 12.17	Antwerp
Eduardo Cruces	Chili	Santiago de Chile	01.17 – 03.17	Antwerp
Tamara Van San	Belgium	Brussels	02.17 – 03.17	Kooshk Residency, Tehran
Leda Bourgogne	Austria	Berlin	04.17 – 06.17	Antwerp
Ada Van Hoorebeke	Belgium	Berlin	04.17 – 06.17	AIR_Frankfurt, Frankfurt am Main
Scott Raby	USA	London	05.17 – 06.17	Antwerp
Paky Vlassopoulou	Greece	Athens	05.17 – 09.17	Antwerp
Luisa Ungar	Columbia	Bogota	06.17 – 11.17	Antwerp

NAME	ORIGIN	CURRENT	PERIOD OF RESIDENCY	RESIDENCY PLACE
Matin Abedi	Iran	Tehran	07.17	Antwerp
Arnaud Eubelen	Belgium	Liège	07.17 – 09.17	Antwerp
Eva L'Hoest	Belgium	Liège	07.17 – 09.17	Antwerp
Lifepatch	Indonesia	Yogjakarta	08.17 – 10.17	Antwerp
Eleanor Wright	United Kingdom	Düsseldorf	08.17 – 10.17	Antwerp
Sam Watson	United Kingdom	Düsseldorf	08.17 – 10.17	Antwerp
Nadia Hebson	United Kingdom	Newcastle	08.17 – 10.17	Antwerp
Paul Becker	United Kingdom	Newcastle	08.17 – 10.17	Antwerp
Koba De Meutter	Belgium	Brussels	09.17 – 10.17	R.A.T, Mexico City
Ciel Grommen	Belgium	Brussels	10.17 – 12.17	R.A.V.I., Liège
Line Boogaerts	Belgium	Mechelen	11.17 – 01.18	Antwerp / Artistes en Résidence, Clermont-Ferrand
Tom Castinel	France	Lyon	11.17 – 01.18	Antwerp / Artistes en Résidence, Clermont-Ferrand
Jeroen Bocken	Belgium	Antwerp	01.18 – 12.18	Antwerp
Chloé Delanghe	Belgium	Brussels	01.18 – 12.18	Antwerp
Ans Mertens	Belgium	Brussels	01.18 – 12.18	Antwerp
Céline Mathieu	Belgium	Antwerp	01.18 – 12.18	Antwerp
Puck Vonk	The Netherlands	Antwerp	01.18 – 12.18	Antwerp

NAME	ORIGIN	CURRENT	PERIOD OF RESIDENCY	RESIDENCY PLACE
Sidney Aelbrecht	Belgium	Antwerp	01.18 – 06.18	Antwerp / MeetFactory Prague
Romana Drdová	Czech Republic	Prague	01.18 – 06.18	Antwerp / MeetFactory Prague
Phumulani Ntuli	South Africa	Johannesburg	01.18 – 03.18	Antwerp
Amir Farsijani	Iran	Tehran	02.18 – 03.18	Antwerp
Saddie Choua	Belgium	Brussels	02.18	Kooshk Residency, Tehran
Koyuki Kazahaya	Japan	Brussels	04.18 – 06.18	AIR_Frankfurt, Frankfurt am Main
Maurice Doherty	Belfast	Berlin	04.18 – 09.18	Antwerp
Ksenija Jovišević	Belgrade	Frankfurt	04.18 – 06.18	Antwerp
Hemant Sareen	India	New Delhi	05.18 – 06.18	Antwerp
Bruno Zhu	Portugal	Amsterdam	06.18 – 09.18	Antwerp
Gary Farrelly	Ireland	Brussels	07.18 – 09.18	Antwerp
Tea Palmelund	Germany	Berlin	07.18 – 09.18	Antwerp
Merle Vorwald	Germany	Berlin	07.18 – 09.18	Antwerp
Janina Warnk	Germany	Cologne	07.18 – 08.18	Antwerp
Meryem Erkus	Germany	Cologne	07.18 – 08.18	Antwerp
Ani Schulze	Germany	Brussels	07.18 – 09.18	R.A.V.I., Liège
Pieter Geenen	Belgium	Brussels	09.18 – 10.18	R.A.T Mexico City
Marc Buchy	France	Brussels	09.18 – 11.18	Lugar A Dudas, Cali

NAME	ORIGIN	CURRENT	PERIOD OF RESIDENCY	RESIDENCY PLACE
Naufus Ramírez -Figueroa	Guatemala	New York	09.18 – 11.18	Antwerp
Ivan Cheng	Australia	Amsterdam	09.18 – 12.18	Antwerp
Sara Giannini	Italy	Amsterdam	09.18 – 12.18	Antwerp
Elvia Teotski	France	Marseille	10.18 – 02.19	Antwerp / Artistes en Résidence, Clermont-Ferrand
Pepa Ivanova	Bulgaria	Ghent	10.18 – 02.19	Antwerp / Artistes en Résidence, Clermont-Ferrand

INDEX OF ACTIVITIES 2013 – 2018

TITLE	WHEN / WHERE	ARTISTS	PARTNERS
AIR Tailor Made	11.01.13 – 08.02.13 / Showroom St Lucas school of arts, Antwerp Borgerhout	Suse Weber	St Lucas / Base Alpha Gallery
AIR Traces presentation	03.04.13 / 98 Weeks Qarantina, Beirut		98 Weeks / NOA Magazine
Hunter	24.08.13 – 03.09.13 / Church of our Lady-across-the-Dyle, Mechelen	Edgardo Aragón	Contour Biënnale
AIR Tailor Made: Bhagwati Prasad	16.10.13 / Lockkeeper's house, Antwerp Harbor	Bhagwati Prasad, Raqs Media Collective	Europalia India
A next stop called hearsing	16.10.13 – 19.10.13 / 98 Weeks and Villa Fleming Qarantina, Beirut	Pedro Barateiro, Amal Dibo, André Romão, Mark Luyten, Marwa Arsanios, Nathan Witt	Kunsthalle Lissabon / 98 Weeks / NOA Magazine
AIR River Bar: Ultra Eczema	06.11.13 / Lockkeeper's house, Antwerp Harbor	Angela Sawyer, Dog Lady Island, Electric Mud, Skin Graft, DJ De Kunst	Scheld'apen
Word of Mouth	21.11.13 / Showroom, St Lucas, Antwerp Borgerhout	Stine Marie Jacobsen	St Lucas School of Art

TITLE	WHEN / WHERE	ARTISTS	PARTNERS
AIR Tailor Made	27.11.13 / Lockkeeper's house, Antwerp Harbor	Bhagwati Prasad	Europalia India
AIR Tailor Made	10.12.13 / Lockkeeper's house, Antwerp Harbor	Mathilde Du Sordet & Kato Six	Artistes en Résidence, Clermont-Ferrand
AIR Tailor Made	22.01.14 / Lockkeeper's house, Antwerp Harbor	Rumiko Hagiwara	
AIR Tailor Made	12.02.14 / Lockkeeper's house, Antwerp Harbor	Reg Carremans	
Het Kanaal / Le Canal	26.02.14 / Lockkeeper's house, Antwerp Harbor	Jonathan De Winter, Xavier Mary	NICC / Espace 251 Nord / R.A.V.I., Liège
Claire Liengme	12.03.14 / Showroom St Lucas, Antwerp Borgerhout	Claire Liengme	St Lucas / Fondation Mercier Sierre / Ecav Sierre
Het Kanaal / Le Canal	26.03.14 / Lockkeeper's house, Antwerp Harbor	Fabian Rouwette, Antoine Van Impe	Espace 251 Nord / R.A.V.I., Liège
Selection of Shorts	27.03.14 / Former store, café and banquethall, Brussels center	Laure Prouvost	Beurs-schouwburg Brussels / Extra City Antwerp

TITLE	WHEN / WHERE	ARTISTS	PARTNERS
Wantee and Grandma's Dreams	04.04.14 – 25.05.14 / Former industrial laundry building, Antwerp Berchem	Laure Prouvost	Extra City Antwerp
AIR Tailor Made	23.04.14 / Lockkeeper's house, Antwerp Harbor	Juha Pekka Matias Laakkonen	M HKA
AIR River Bar: Ruderalia	26.04.14 / Lockkeeper's house, Antwerp Harbor	Vibracathedral Orchestra, WR Ravenveer, Huur is Duur, Nathalie Forget, Astral Social Club, Blaastaal, Joris De Rycke, Diane Rabreau	KRAAK
AIR Tailor Made	21.05.14 / Lockkeeper's house, Antwerp Harbor	Augustas Serapinas	M HKA
From Wantee to Some Signs	14.06 / Former industrial laundry building, Antwerp Berchem	Laure Prouvost	Extra City Antwerp
Het Kanaal / Le Canal	15.06.14 – 10.08.14 / former industrial laundry building, Antwerp Berchem	Antoine Van Impe, Fabian Rouwette, Jonathan De Winter, Kasper Bosmans, Philippe Van Wolputte, Elise Eeraerts, Thomas Grødal, Xavier Mary	Espace 251 Nord / NICC / Extra City

TITLE	WHEN / WHERE	ARTISTS	PARTNERS
AIR Traces: Austruweel	06.09.14 – 05.10.14 / Lockkeeper's house, customs house, porter's lodge at the pumphouse, houseboat, chippy	Bisan Abu-Eisheh, Mounira Al Solh, Paul Becker, Jonathan De Winter, Reg Carremans, Chloé Dierckx, Laurent Dupont-Garitte, Carla Filipe, Shaun Gladwell, Stine Marie Jacobsen, Ria Pacquée, Karl Philips, Savage, Dennis Tyfus	
AIR Tailor Made	17.09.14 / Customs house, Antwerp harbor	Carla Filipe	
AIR Tailor Made	24.09.14 / Houseboat, Antwerp harbor	Savage	
AIR Tailor Made	02.10.14 / Porter's lodge at the pump house, Antwerp harbor	Stine Marie Jacobsen	
De Sokkel #8	05.10.14 – 05.04.15 / City Park, Antwerp	Nicholas Hoffman	Middelheim Museum
Het Kanaal / Le Canal	25.10.14 – 29.11.14 / former administrative center of a colemine, Liège	Antoine Van Impe, Fabian Rouwette, Jonathan De Winter, Kasper Bosmans, Philippe Van Wolputte, Elise Eeraerts, Thomas Grødal, Xavier Mary	Espace 251 Nord / NICC
XIX	30.10.14 – 09.11.14 / former hotel Silvana, Frankfurt Bahnhofsviertel	Ignace Cami, Gabriela Gonzalez, Philip Janssens, Saori Kuno, Siet Raeymaekers, Tim Segers, Bart Van Dijck, Bear Bones Lay Low, Griesbacher, Saul Judd, curated by Bert Jacobs	Kulturbunker Frankfurt / basis e.v. Frankfurt

TITLE	WHEN / WHERE	ARTISTS	PARTNERS
AIR Tailor Made	12.11.14 / Lockkeeper's house, Antwerp harbor	Simon Feydieu, Joris De Rycke	Artistes en Résidence, Clermont-Ferrand
AIR River Bar: Midnight 3000	12.12.14 / Lockkeeper's house, Antwerp harbor	Bert Jacobs, DJ Meeuw, Orphan Fairytale, Blodfet & Dj Lonely, Mr Vast, DJ SoFa, Chris Ferreira, Asuna, The Absolute End	
AIR Tailor Made	30.01.15 / Former shop, Antwerp Borgerhout	Stefanie Pretnar	Heimat project space / Antwerp Art Weekend
STRT Kit #1	30.01.15 / Former garage, Antwerp Borgerhout	Daan Gielis, Elise Eeraerts, Jane Coppin, Karolien Chromiak, Lore Van Roelen	Studio Start / Antwerp Art Weekend
Lodgers #1: MER Paper Kunsthalle	31.01.15 – 19.04.15 / Former grain storage, Antwerp South	MER Paper Kunsthalle, Ania Soliman, Sigtryggur Berg Sigmarsson	M HKA
AIR Tailor Made	25.03.15 – 27.03.15 / Former garage Antwerp Borgerhout	Nihan Somay	Sint Lucas School of Arts / Antwerp, Fondation Mercier, Sierre
Mann beißt Hund	28.03.15 – 27.05.15 / 19th century warehouse, historic center Kopenhagen	Stine Marie Jacobsen	Overgaden Contemporary Art Institute / Danish Art Foundation
audioMER. Lp release	29.03.15 / Former grain storage, Antwerp South	Aki Onda, Mauro Antonio Pawlowski & Sigtryggur Berg Sigmarsson, Anne-Mie an Kerckhoven, Jack Allett	M HKA

TITLE	WHEN / WHERE	ARTISTS	PARTNERS
Lodgers #1	09.04.15 / Former grain storage, Antwerp South	Ania Soliman	M HKA
STRT Kit #1: presentation Beirut	27.04.15 / Former house, Qarantina, Beirut	Daan Gielis, Jane Coppin, Lore Van Roelen, Karolien Chromiak	Villa Fleming, Mounira Al Solh
LODGERS #2: Daemons & Shell Scripts	01.05.15 – 05.07.15 / Former grain storage, Antwerp South; house, Berchem; lockkeeper's house, Antwerp Harbour	bolwerK with Axoloti, Artan Balaj, Ash Bowland, Jo Caimo, Tina Cake Line, Hou Chien Cheng, Jurgen Desmet, Domestic Science Club, Ana Dragic, GIRLSLIKEUS, Erin Helsen, Heimat, Hello Shelly, Paul Hendrikse, Pieter Heremans, Pepa Ivanova, Shelbatra Jashari, Saori Kuno, Adisak Jirasakkasem, Karin Orisa, Margareth Kaserere, KD85, Lokaal 01, MADmoizel, Enad Marouf, Donna Metzlar, Samyra Moumouh, Danny Neyman, Oona Prinsen, Tara Pattenden, Pinatpechblenda, Phantom Chips, Natacha Roussel, Planète Concrète, Femke Snelting, Skybox, Strangelove, Isabel Tesfazghi, Katerina Undo, Marthe Van Dessel, Wendy Van Wynsberghe, Lize Verlooy, Caroline Vincart, V+S, Sophie Anson & Veronik Willems, Wireless Antwerpen, Chantal Yzermans, Adva Zakai, 3dee,…	M HKA
AIR River Bar: An event on the exotic	24.05.15 / Lockkeeper's house, Antwerp harbour	Mike Cooper, Kink Gong, Lieven Martens Moana, Bear Bones Lay Low, Korla Documentary	KRAAK
The world is inside of it. The world is around it, publication	07.05.15	Mathilde Du Sordet	Artistes en Résidence, Clermont-Ferrand

TITLE	WHEN / WHERE	ARTISTS	PARTNERS
Finissage Lodgers #2 Daemons and shell scripts	11.07.15 / Lockkeeper's house, Antwerp harbour	A'lies van Wonderland, Lady Doublet, Phantom Chips, Planète Concrète, Miss Schwarzkopf, Sir Edward, ON3MCR	M HKA / Strangelove Festival
AIR Tailor Made	26.08.15 / Lockkeeper's house, Antwerp harbour	Pieter Huybrechts, Maryam Ashkanian	Kooshk Residency Tehran
Wrijving van Gedachten	20.09.15 – 14.02.16 / Former house of Vincent Van Gogh	Lieven Segers, Nel Aerts, Lennart Lahuis, Niek Hendrix	Van Gogh Huis Zundert / BesteBuren
De Sokkel #10	10.10.15 – 09.03.16 / City Park, Antwerp Center	Yan Tomaszewski	Middelheim Museum
Lodgers #3: Apparent Extent	01.08.15 – 30.10.15 / Former grain storage, Antwerp South	Apparent Extent with Johanna Billing, Mika Taanila, Christina Jendreiko, Kallabris, Franziska Windisch, Volker Zander, hobbypop-MUSEUM, Beaster, A. U. Awings Unlimited	M HKA
STRT Kit #1: No Blossom No Moonlight	12.09.15 – 06.12.15 / former industrial laundry building Antwerp Berchem	Karolien Chromiak, Jane Coppin Elise Eeraerts, Daan Gielis, Lore Van Roelen, curated by: Kunsthalle Lissabon	Studio Start / Extra City
Dünya Döner	23.10.15 / Museum	Serra Tansel	Europalia Turkey / MAS

TITLE	WHEN / WHERE	ARTISTS	PARTNERS
Livro de Todo o Universo (Chopped and Screwed)	08.11.15 / The corrector's room in the 16th century printing house of Plantin Moretus, Antwerp center	Bianca Baldi	Museum Plantijn Moretus
AIR Tailor Made	26.11.15 / Lockkeeper's house, Antwerp harbor	Baptiste Croze, Lodewijk Heylen	Artistes en Résidence, Clermont-Ferrand
10 Stories of a Journey publication	06.12.15 / Former industrial laundry building, Antwerp Berchem	Karolien Chromiak, Jane Coppin, Elise Eeraerts, Daan Gielis, Lore Van Roelen, Anne-Marie Poels, John C Welchman, Fadi Tofeili, Alan Quireyns, Luis Silva & João Mourão, Dorian Van der Brempt, Greet Vlegels	Studio Start / Extra City
Lodgers #4: School of Missing Studies	31.10.15 – 17.01.16 / Former grain storage, Antwerp South	School of Missing Studies with Shippr, Christian Hansen, Jeroen Verbeeck, Allan Sekula, Martin Schepers, Dirk Van Lieshout, Kees Brouwer, Common Room, Tom Fassaert, Wiebe Eekman	M HKA
AIR Tailor Made	16.12.15 / Lockkeeper's house, Antwerp harbor	Elise Eeraerts, Lennart Lahuis	Van Goghhouse Zundert / Studio Start
Staat van de Stad / State of the City / Zustand der Stadt	04.01.16 – 18.12.16 / Lockkeeper's house, Antwerp harbour; former customs house, Rotterdam harbor; former hotel Silvana, Frankfurt Bahnhofsviertel	Ghislain Amar, Levent Kunt, Karl Philips, Ani Schulze, Stijn Van Dorpe, Mirte Van Duppen	Basis e.v. Frankfurt am Main / AIR_Frankfurt; Paviljoen a/h Water / Rotterdam; Frankfurter Buchmesse 2016

TITLE	WHEN / WHERE	ARTISTS	PARTNERS
Image Generator II	05.02.16 – 28.02.16 / Former industrial laundry building, Antwerp Berchem	Bianca Baldi	Extra City
The Boogeyman exhibition and publication	02.03.16 – 27.04.16 / Former shop, Antwerp Center	Yan Tomaszewski with Karel Tuytschaever, Jack Davey, Michaël Smits, Alan Quireyns	Catapult / Middelheim Museum
Lodgers #5: KatSalon	03.03.16 – 17.04.16 / Former grain storage, Antwerp South	Le Salon with François Curlet, John M Armleder, Laetitia Chauvin, Amanda Ross-Ho, Poesivski Poeselovski, Eric Croes	M HKA
A one-night show	16.03.16 / Lockkeeper's house, Antwerp harbour	Niek Hendrix, Lennart Lahuis, Lieven Segers, Children of the White Leaf, Pinkhouse Bar, Victoria Wigzell, Alice De Mont, Nel Aerts, Floris Vanhoof, Bart Sloow, Dubais, Dj's Cosmo Knex, Zoot Ruff Ski, Chinese Takeaway, Robert Šalanda, Pierre Berthet	Pinkhouse
Rouge Belge	23.03.16 / Former garage, Antwerp Borgerhout	Victoria Wigzell	Sint Lucas School of Arts Antwerp / Fondation Mercier Sierre
Lodgers #6: Ultra Eczema	30.04.16 – 24.07.16 / former grain storage, Antwerp South	Peter Fengler, Caned Icoda, Albert Mayr, Menstruation Sisters, Dennis Tyfus	M HKA
Opening new location	18.05.16 / Former officer's houses, Antwerp Brederode	Alberto García del Castillo, Ani Schulze, Jim Campers, Luis Lázaro Matos, Mirte Van Duppen, Maika Garnica, mountaincutters, Ode de Kort, Timo Van Grinsven	Studio Start

TITLE	WHEN / WHERE	ARTISTS	PARTNERS
Selected video's	20.07.16 / The Living Room, Former officer's houses, Antwerp Brederode	Serra Tansel, Alexis Lagimodière-Grisé, Asli Baykal, Ingrid Berthon-Moine, Ryan Foerster, Duane Linklater, Daniella Russo, Senar, Eiko Soga, Duval Timoty	
Lodgers #7: Lonelyfingers	07.08.16 – 15.10.16 / former grain storage Antwerp South	Diango Hernandez, Anna Pöhlmann	M HKA
Peeks of Past Sheets of Present	21.08.16 – 24.08.16 / former gasoline station on the highway between Liège and Seraing	Alexis Lagimodière-Grisé	Diesel Project Space
Peeks of present Sheets of past	25.08.16 – 28.08.16 / The Living Room, Former officer's houses, Antwerp Brederode	Alexis Lagimodière-Grisé	Diesel Project Space
AIR Tailor Made	30.08.16 / The Living Room, Former officer's houses, Antwerp Brederode	Gauthier Oushoorn, Roya Keshavarz	Kooshk Residency, Tehran
Lines of Flight	04.09.16 – 16.09.16 / The Living Room	Jayne Dent, Alexis Lagimodière-Grisé, Chantal Peñalosa, Marie Zolamian	Open Studios 2016

TITLE	WHEN / WHERE	ARTISTS	PARTNERS
STRT Kit #2: In the wake of his surrounding, he fades	09.09.16 – 25.09.16 / Former industrial laundry building, Antwerp Berchem	Jim Campers, Maika Garnica, mountaincutters, Ode de Kort, Timo Van Grinsven, curated by: FormContent	Studio Start / Extra City / Kunsthart
Lodgers #8: Pages	30.10.16 – 22.01.17 / former grain storage, Antwerp South	Babak Afrassiabi, Nesrin Tabatabai	M HKA
A hand in wet concrete, a foot in the sea and all things between are between you and me	27.09.16 / The Living Room	Jayne Dent	Newcastle University
The Hermitage Artist Retreat	01.11.16 – 11.12.16 / Hermitage Artist Retreat Florida	Daan Gielis	Stad Antwerpen
AIR Tailor Made	08.11.16 / The Living Room	Chantal Peñalosa	
AIR Tailor Made	16.12.16 / The Living Room	Ode de Kort & Maika Garnica with Chakky Kato, Senne Claes, Cuntst, De Batteries	
Catalogue release: State of the City	16.12.16 / Former Hotel Silviana, Bahnhofsviertel Frankfurt am Main	Ghislain Amar, Ani Schulze, Karl Philips, Levent Kunt, Mirte Van Duppen, Stijn Van Dorpe, Wim van der Celen, Ina Hartwig, Dirk Hülstrunk, Maarten Inghels, Hester Knibbe, Kathrin Meyer, Bart Moeyaert, Christin Müller, Ine Pisters, Alan Quireyns, Felix Ruhöfer, Kamiel Verschueren	basis e.v. Frankfurt am Main

TITLE	WHEN / WHERE	ARTISTS	PARTNERS
La Grange	22.02.17 / The Living Room	Nicolas Valckenaere	
Crox 538	25.02.17 / Former brewery	Tomáš Kajánek	Croxhapox
The Living Room: Elen Braga	08.03.17 / The Living Room	Elen Braga	
[Resonating Spaces], The value of residencies and workspaces in Belgium and the Netherlands	16.03.17 / LUCA School of Arts, Campus Brussels	Philippine Hoegen, Taru Elfving, Hebe Verstappen, Samira Boon, Caroline Dumalin, Ghislaine Leung	Creative Industries Fund in the Netherlands / Flanders Arts Institute / Frans Masereel Center / LUCA School of Arts / Platform Werkplaatsen
The Living Room: Stijn Van Dorpe & Tomáš Kajánek	22.03.17 / The Living Room	Stijn Van Dorpe, Tomáš Kajánek	MeetFactory, Prague
Lodgers #9: Hotel Charleroi, From HERE to THERE – part 1	02.04.17 / Former grain storage, Antwerp South	Johanna Tinzl, Philippe S3 BelGenion, Serge Stephan, Claude Cattelain, Adrien Tirtiaux, Cäcilia Brown	M HKA
The Living Room: Liesbet Grupping	25.04.17 / The Living Room	Liesbet Grupping	Artistes en Résidence, Clermont-Ferrand

TITLE	WHEN / WHERE	ARTISTS	PARTNERS
Lodgers #9: Hotel Charleroi, From HERE to THERE – part 2	27.04.17 / Former grain storage, Antwerp South	Anna Witt, Annabel Lange, Antoine Turillon, Adrien Tirtiaux / Claude Cattelain, Baptiste Elbaz, Cäcilia Brown, Hannes Zebedin, Johanna Tinzl, Philippe S3 BelGenion, Maria Giovanna Drago & Sophie Thun, Manfred Pernice, Sébastien Lacombez, Serge Stephan, Stijn Van Dorpe, The Mental Masonry Lab	M HKA
Book Launch Merman	14.05.17 / Former shop, Brussels central station	Alberto García del Castillo	Etablissement d'en face
Antwerp Art Weekend	19.05.17 – 21.05.17 / The Living Room	Leda Bourgogne, Paky Vlassopoulou, Luisa Ungar	
Lodgers #10: Jubilee	19.05.17 – 23.07.17 / former grain storage, Antwerp South	Philippe Thomas, Agency, Patrick Bernier & Olive Martin, Antony Hudek, Judith Ickowicz, Sven Lütticken, Daniel mcClean, Julia Wielgus, Steyn Bergs, Florence Cheval, Sari Depreeuw, Scott Raby, Sara Martinetti, Carey Young	M HKA
The Living Room: Leda Bourgogne	07.06.17 / The Living Room	Leda Bourgogne	AIR_Frankfurt
The Living Room: Luisa Ungar	21.06.17 / Thc Living Room	Luisa Ungar	
The Living Room: STRT Kit #1 – #3	28.06.17 – 05.07.17 / The Living Room	Polien Boons, Kitty Kamp, Karen Moser, Amber Vanluffelen, Mathieu Verhaeghe	Studio Start
The Living Room: Eva L'Hoest & Arnaud Eubelen	19.07.17 / The Living Room	Eva L'Hoest, Arnaud Eubelen	R.A.V.I. Liège / Espace 251 Nord, Liège

TITLE	WHEN / WHERE	ARTISTS	PARTNERS
The Living Room: Matin Abedi & Tamara Van San	26.07.17 / The Living Room	Matin Abedi, Tamara Van San	Kooshk Residency, Tehran
Book Launch L.A. Magazine	16.08.17 / The Living Room	Xavier Mary, Noëmi Merca, André Piguet, Arnaud Eubelen, Benny Van den Meulengracht-Vrancx, The Garden Ceremony, Alex Morrison, Eva L'Hoest, Kasper Bosmans, La Superette, Ciel Grommen, Alexis Lagimodière-Grisé, Oscar Hugal, Benoit Platéus, Ria Pacquée, Marie Zolamian	Espace 251 Nord / Diesel Project Space
Lodgers #11: Drop City	18.08.17 – 15.10.17 / Former grain storage, Antwerp South	Paul Becker, Francesco Pedraglio, Natasha Soobramanien, Luke Williams, Nadia Hebson, Hana Leaper, August Luke McCreadie, Anna Barham, Tess Denman-Cleaver, Titania Seidl, Ellen Lesperance, Daniela Cascella, Giovanna Zapperi, Rubén Grillo, Christian Jendreiko, Marku Karstiess, Metaphysics VR, Pentecostal Party, Suzanna Pezo, Luisa Ungar, Jani Ruscica, Deanna Smith, Paky Vlassopoulou, Eleanor Wright	M HKA
The Living Room XL	02.09.17 / BODEM, a public garden with summer bar around the residency	Allon Kaye, Amber Vanluffelen, Arnaud Eubelen, Aymeric De Tapol, Eva L'Hoest, Jelle Spruyt, Jurgen Ots, Kitty Kamp, Koba De Meutter, Nicolas Valckenaere, Paky Vlassopoulou, Razen, Rowan Van As, Stijn Van Dorpe, Wim Catrysse	Studio Start / Brandt / Provincie Antwerpen / Stad Antwerpen
The Tale of Tiger and Lion	12.10.17 – 07.01.18 / Former grain storage, Antwerp South	Lifepatch Collective	Europalia Indonesia / M HKA

TITLE	WHEN / WHERE	ARTISTS	PARTNERS
STRT Kit #3: Brief Flashes against a world	20.10.17 – 11.11.17 / Former industrial laundry building, Antwerp Berchem	Amber Vanluffelen, Karen Moser, Kitty Kamp, Mathieu Verhaeghe, Polien Boons, curated by: Övül Ö. Durmusoglu	Studio Start / Extra City / Kunsthart
I like to confuse them when they're trying to understand	15.11.17 / Cinema Zuid	Luisa Ungar, Oscar Ruiz Navia, Simón Mesa Soto, Luis Ospina y Carlos Mayolo	Cinema Zuid
Lodgers #12: APE, opening and performance	16.11.17 / Former grain storage, Antwerp South	Arnout & Michiel De Cleene, Pieterjan Ginckels, Manor Grunewald, Hana Miletić	M HKA
The Living Room: Koba De Meutter	07.02.17 / The Living Room	Koba De Meutter	R.A.T. Mexico City
Meet the artists: Saddie Choua & Amir Farsijani	14.03.18 / Fine Arts Palace of Victor Horta, Brussels central station	Saddie Choua, Amir Farsijani	BOZAR / Kooshk Residency / EUNIC
Book launch Wrijving van Gedachten	22.03.18 / Former grain storage, Antwerp South	Nel Aerts, Lieven Segers, Lennart Lahuis, Niek Hendrix	Van Goghhuis
The__bends in the wrong direction. Episode 2. Chapter One	27.03.18 – 30.03.18 / Former garage, Antwerp Borgerhout	Phumulani Ntuli	St Lucas School of Arts Antwerp / ECAV Sierre
The Living Room: Romana Drdová & Sidney Aelbrecht	28.03.18 / The Living Room	Romana Drdová, Sidney Aelbrecht	MeetFactory

TITLE	WHEN / WHERE	ARTISTS	PARTNERS
Mamarat (Paths) residency Ramallah	01.04.18 / Municipality of Ramallah		Ramallah Municipality / Qalandiya International / Qattan Foundation
Antwerp Art Weekend	25.05.18 – 28.05.18 / The Living Room	Maurice Doherty, Ksenija Jovišević	
Een kraai kraait niet maar krast	06.06.18 / The Living Room	Jeroen Bocken	Studio Start
Lodgers #14: ARIA, Royal Conservatoire	31.03.18 – 21.04.18 / Former grain storage, Antwerp South	Tone Brulin, Katharina Smets, Inne Eysermans, Ingrid Leonard	M HKA
Lodgers #14: ARIA, St Lucas School of Art	23.04.18 – 28.04.18 21.05.18 – 09.06.18 / Former grain storage, Antwerp South	Esther Venrooy, Timo Van Grinsven, Bart Lodewijks, Laetitia Gendre	M HKA
Lodgers #14: ARIA, Royal Academy of the Arts	30.04.18 – 20.05.18 / Former grain storage, Antwerp South	Nico Dockx, Mashid Mohadjerin, Vijai Patchineelam, Hemant Sareen, Geert Goiris	M HKA
Lodgers #14: ARIA, CCQC, Wellness Centre Future Proof	10.06.18 – 24.06.18 / Former grain storage, Antwerp South	Arne Herman, Guiliana Ciancio, Hanka Otte, Juna Canela Claver, Karina Beumer, Katinka de Jonge, Lara Garcia Diaz, Liesje De Laet, Louis Volont, Pascal Gielen, Thijs Lijster, Walter van Andel	M HKA

TITLE	WHEN / WHERE	ARTISTS	PARTNERS
Dog.Rooster. Pig	20.06.18 / The Living Room	Céline Mathieu	Studio Start
as i walk at leisure	04.07.18 / The Living Room	Ans Mertens	Studio Start
So That Afternoon, book launch	05.07.18 / Former butcher, Antwerp South	Koba De Meutter	LLS Paleis / Posture Editions
Free flow square yellow – graphical notation for performance	18.07.18 / The Living Room	Puck Vonk	Studio Start
The Living Room: Maika Garnica, Amber Vanluffelen	25.07.18 / The Living Room	Amber Vanluffelen, Maika Garnica	
The Living Room: Specks of blue	01.08.18 / The Living Room	Chloé Delanghe	Studio Start
Lodgers #15: baumusik	02.08 – 01.09	Timothy Shearer, Janina Warnk, Benjamin Adams, Jonas Bruns, Marie Claire Delarber, Meryem Erkus, Lukas Goersmeyer, Echo Ho, Sebastian Ingenhoff, Caroline Kox, Malo, Jan-Ole Schiemann, Britta Terkotte, Roland Kaiser Wilhelm, Eliza Ballesteros & David Lichtner, Pia Bergerbusch, Julia Bünnagel, Berta Valin Escofet, Sebastian Fritzsch, Philipp Hoening, Julia König, Florian Kuhlmann, Carmen Lenhart, Finn Wagner, CAMP INC, Koxette, Liberty Snake, zo-on slows, UMMN, Jeandado, Hall&Rauch, O Pan, Abel, Monibi, Igor Amore, Minjung Cho, Diana Jones, BritKat, Malo	M HKA

TITLE	WHEN / WHERE	ARTISTS	PARTNERS
Speed Core Jour Fixes	08.08 / 15.08 / 22.08 / 29.08 / The Living Room	Merle Vorwald, Tea Palmelund	Encore
The Cabinet of Traces	02.09.18 / The Living Room	Fritz Welch, Malthe Stigaard, Caner Aslan, Nina Könnemann, Arin Rungjang, Ella de Burca, Ryan Siegan-Smith, André Romão, Mounira Al Solh, Francesc Ruiz, Pedro Barateiro, Philip Janssens, Darren Roshier, Ilaria Lupo, Naneci Yurdagül, Post Brothers, Stine Marie Jacobsen, Bhagwati Prasad, Rumiko Hagiwara, Mathilde Du Sordet, Harry Heirmans, Claire Liengme, Fabian Rouwette, Antoine Van Impe, Laure Prouvost, Nicholas Hoffman, Savage, Shaun Gladwell, Dennis Tyfus, Laurent Dupont, Simon Feydieu, Joris De Rycke, Rasmus Søndergaard Johanssen, Yan Tomaszewski, Serra Tansel, Baptiste Croze, Mike Cooper, Reg Carremans, Edgardo Aragón, Bianca Baldi, Victoria Wigzell, Luis Lázaro Matos, Lennart Lahuis, Lodewijk Heylen, Alberto García del Castillo, Ani Schulze, Mirte Van Duppen, Alice De Mont, Alexis Lagimodière-Grisé, Ania Soliman, Bisan Abu-Eisheh, Augustas Serapinas, Stefanie Pretnar, Chantal Peñalosa, Elen Braga, Pages, Leda Bourgogne, Paky Vlassopoulou, Lifepatch, Tom Castinel, Sidney Aelbrecht, Eva L'Hoest, Line Boogaerts, Ksenija Jovisevic, Bruno Zhu, Tomáš Kajánek, Arnaud Eubelen, Stijn Van Dorpe, Hemant Sareen, Maurice Doherty, Luisa Ungar, Liesbet Grupping, Amir Farsijani	Open Studios

TITLE	WHEN / WHERE	ARTISTS	PARTNERS
The Living Room: Gary Farrelly	26.09.18 / The Living Room	Gary Farrelly	R.A.V.I., Liège
Is it dark?	27.09.18 – 30.09.18 / Art center Het Bos, Antwerp skippers quarters	Ekaterina Burlyga, Johannes Büttner, Bastian Hagedorn, Bianca Ludewig, Henrike Naumann, Tea Palmelund, Merle Vorwarld, Marco Buetikofer, Lotte Meret Effinger, Florian Meyer	Het Bos
Lodgers #16: heterotropics	15.09.18 – 16.12.18 / former grain storage, Antwerp South	Sara Giannini, Ivan Cheng, Milena Bonilla, Luisa Ungar	M HKA
STRT Kit #4: We're this and we're that, aren't we	22.09.18 – 14.10.18	Jeroen Bocken, Chloë Delanghe, Céline Mathieu, Ans Mertens, Puck Vonck	Studio Start / Extra City / Kunsthart
Qalandiya International	02.10.18 – 10.10.18 / Ramallah	Ika Sienckiwicz-Novacka, Juka Laakkonen, Alan Quireyns	HIAP Helsinki / Ramallah Muncipality / Qattan Foundation / Qalandiya International / Center for Contemporary Art Ujazdowski Castle Warsaw
Playground Festival	15.11.18 – 17.11.18	Naufus Ramírez-Figueroa	Museum M